THE SCOTTISH FAIRY BOOK

ILLUS-TRATIONS BY MORRIS MEREDITH WILLIAMS

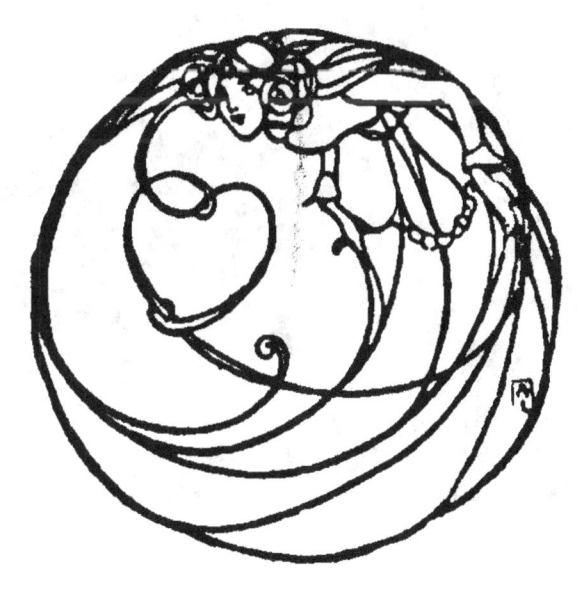

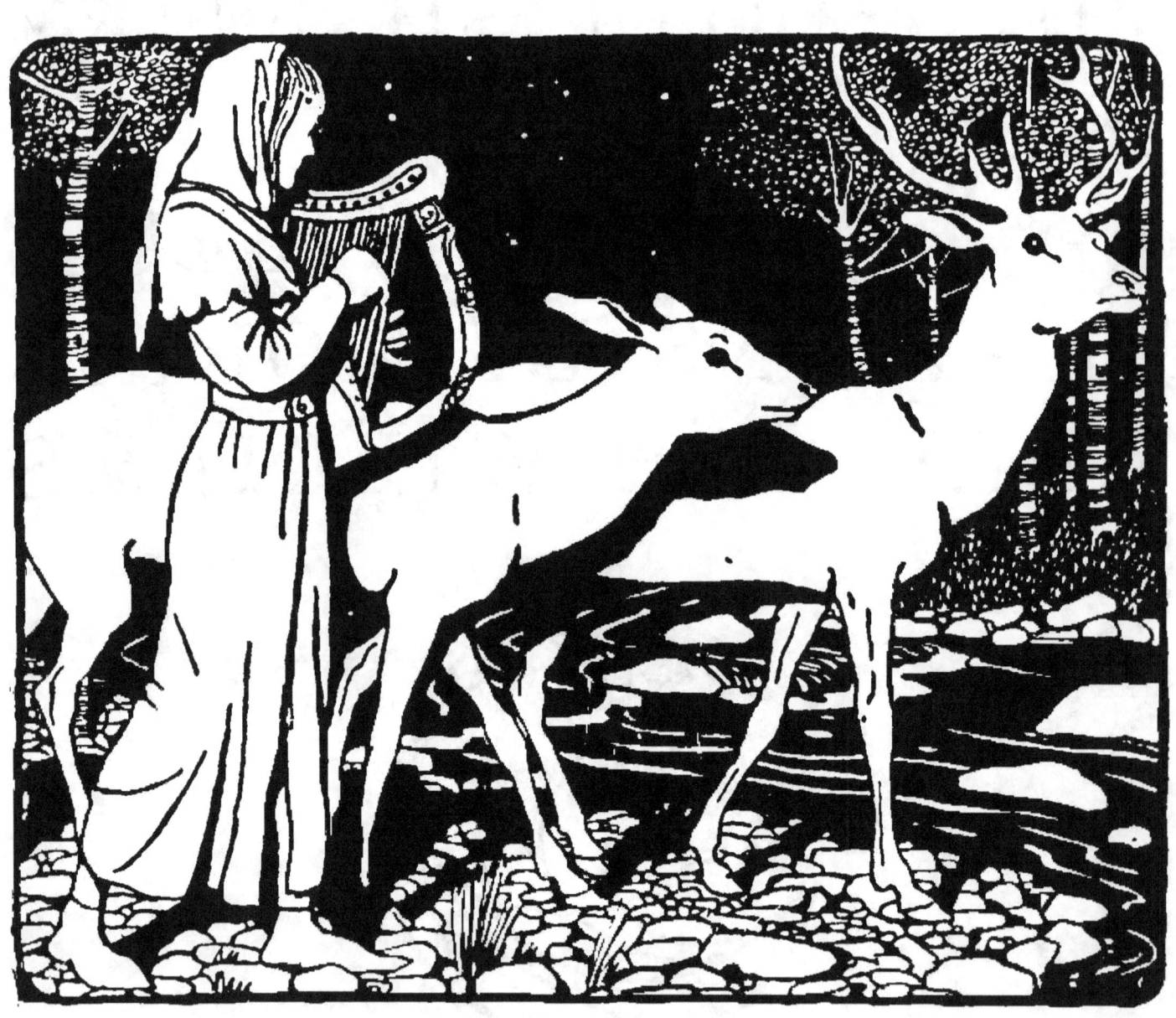

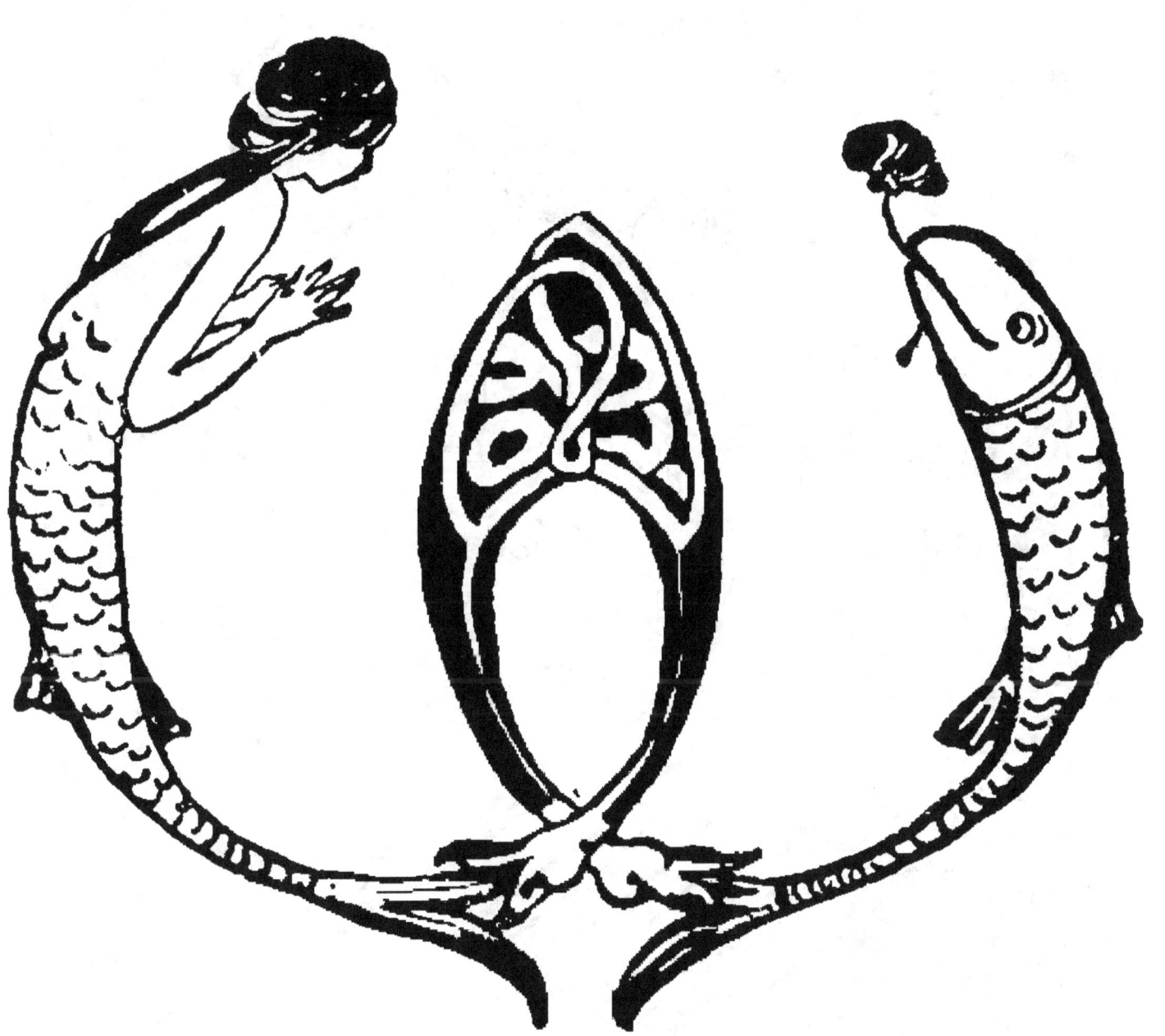

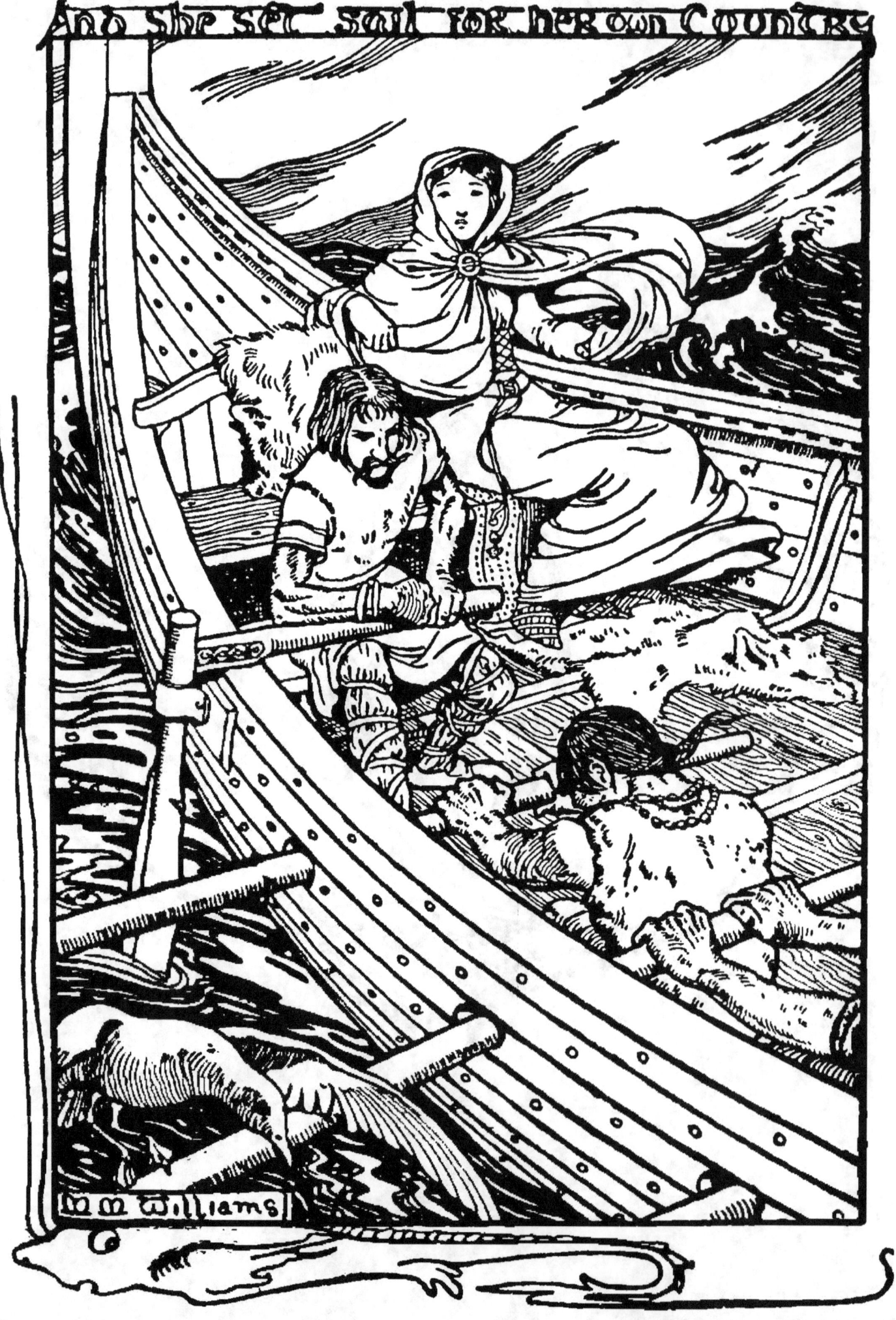

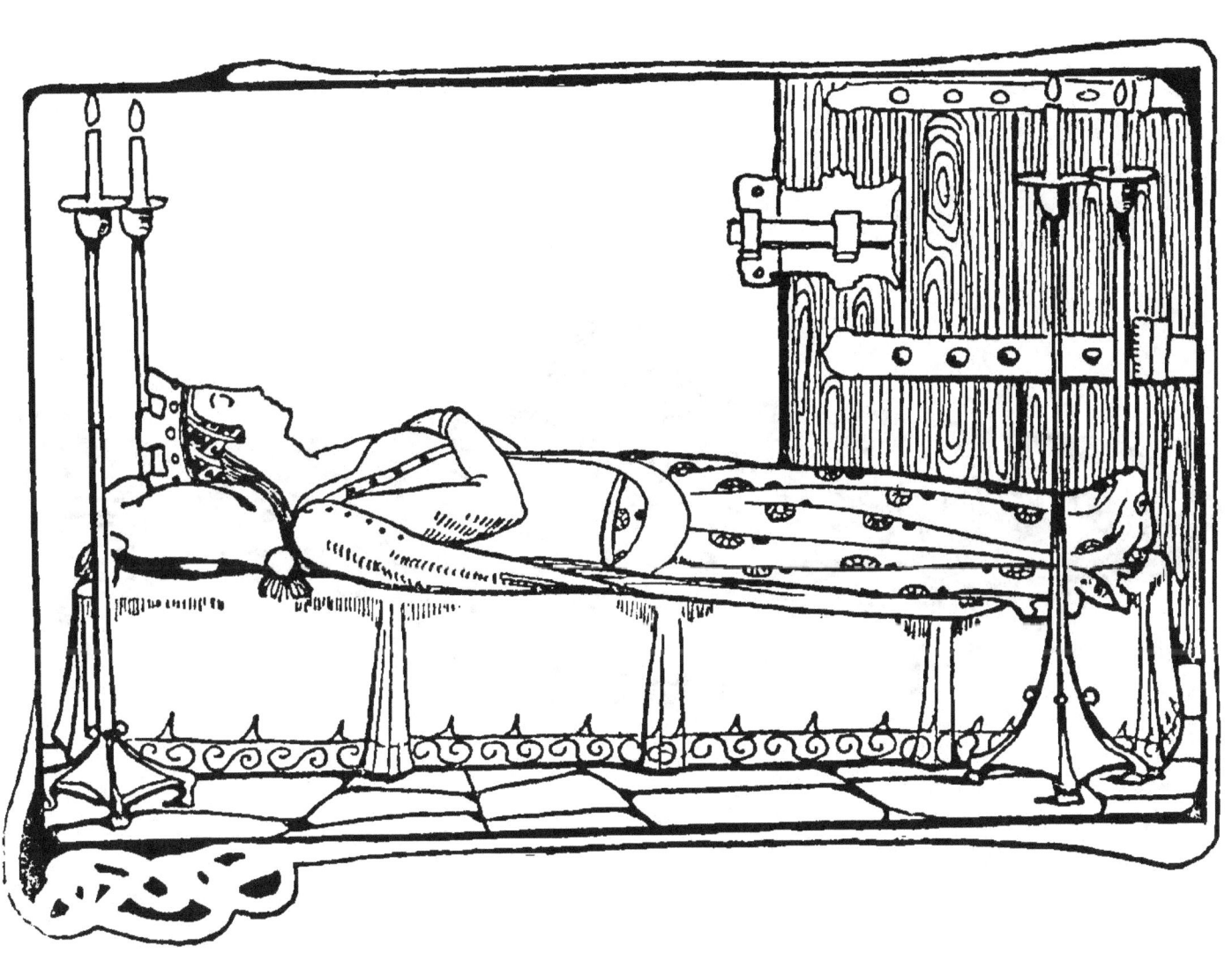

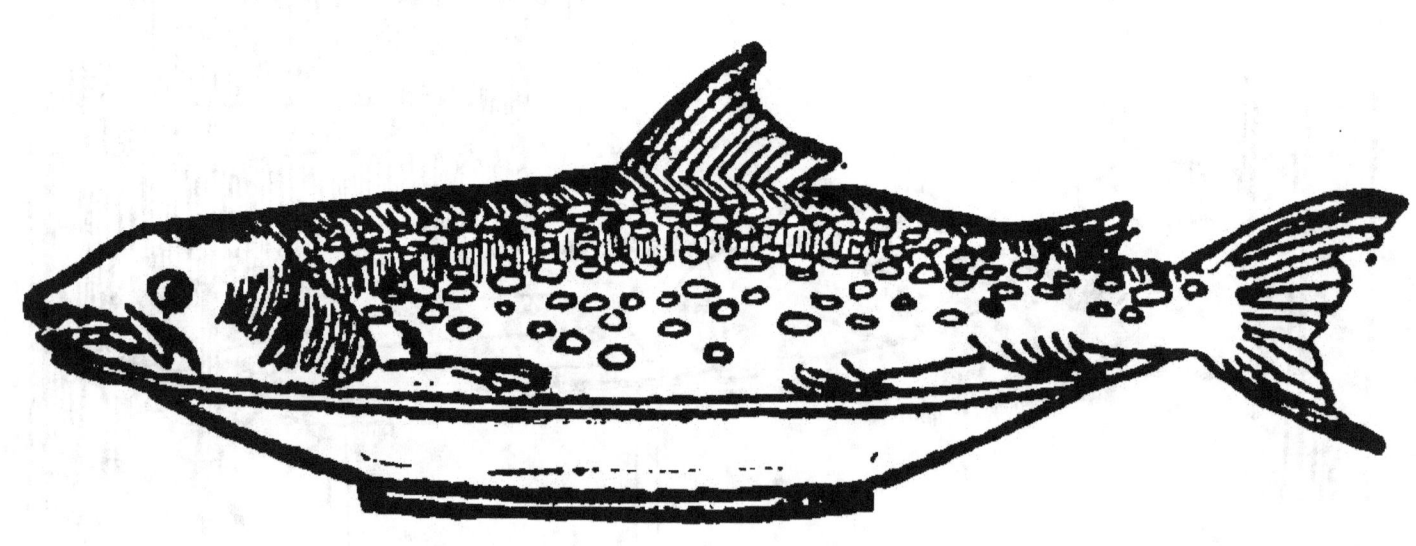

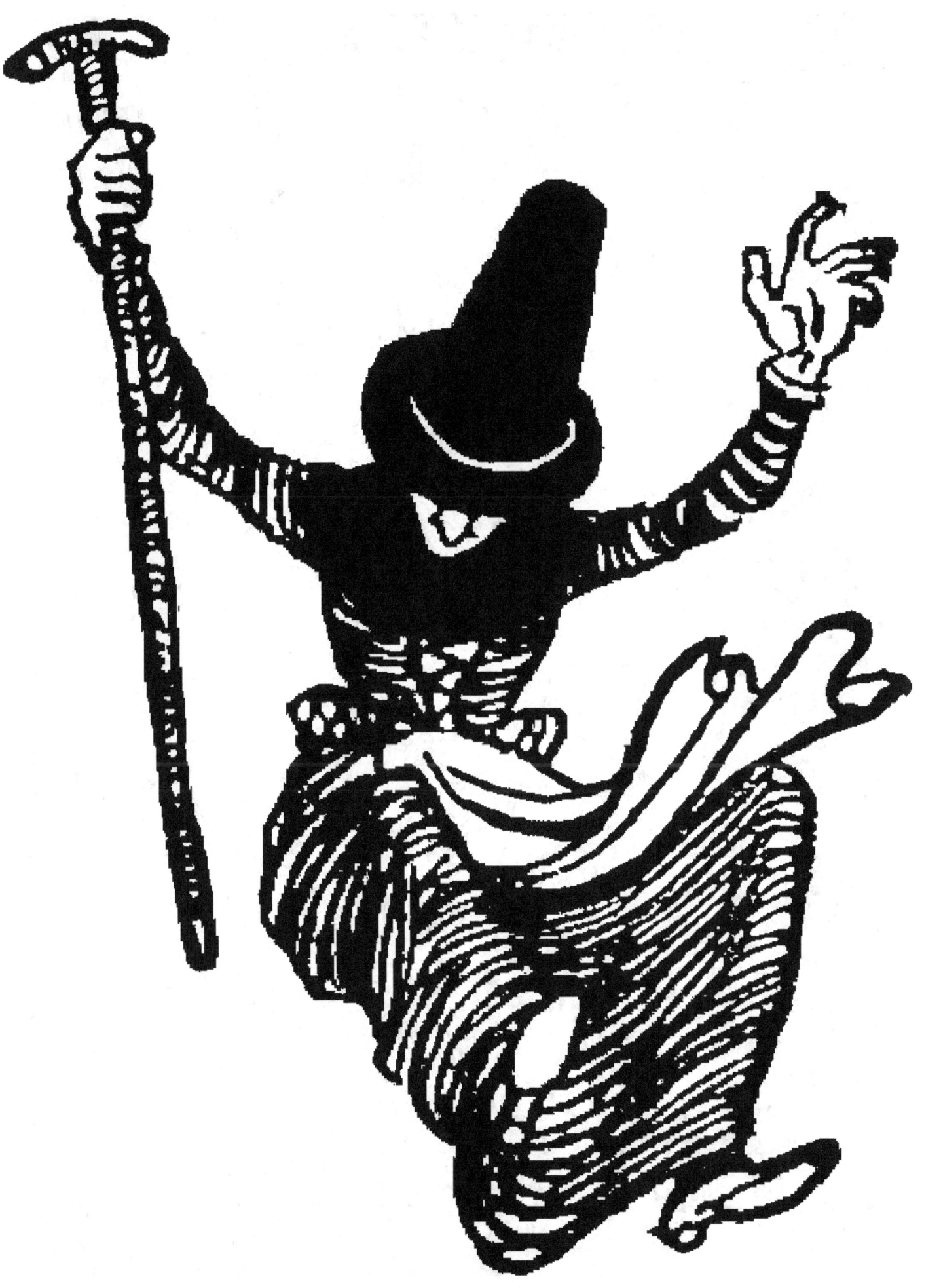

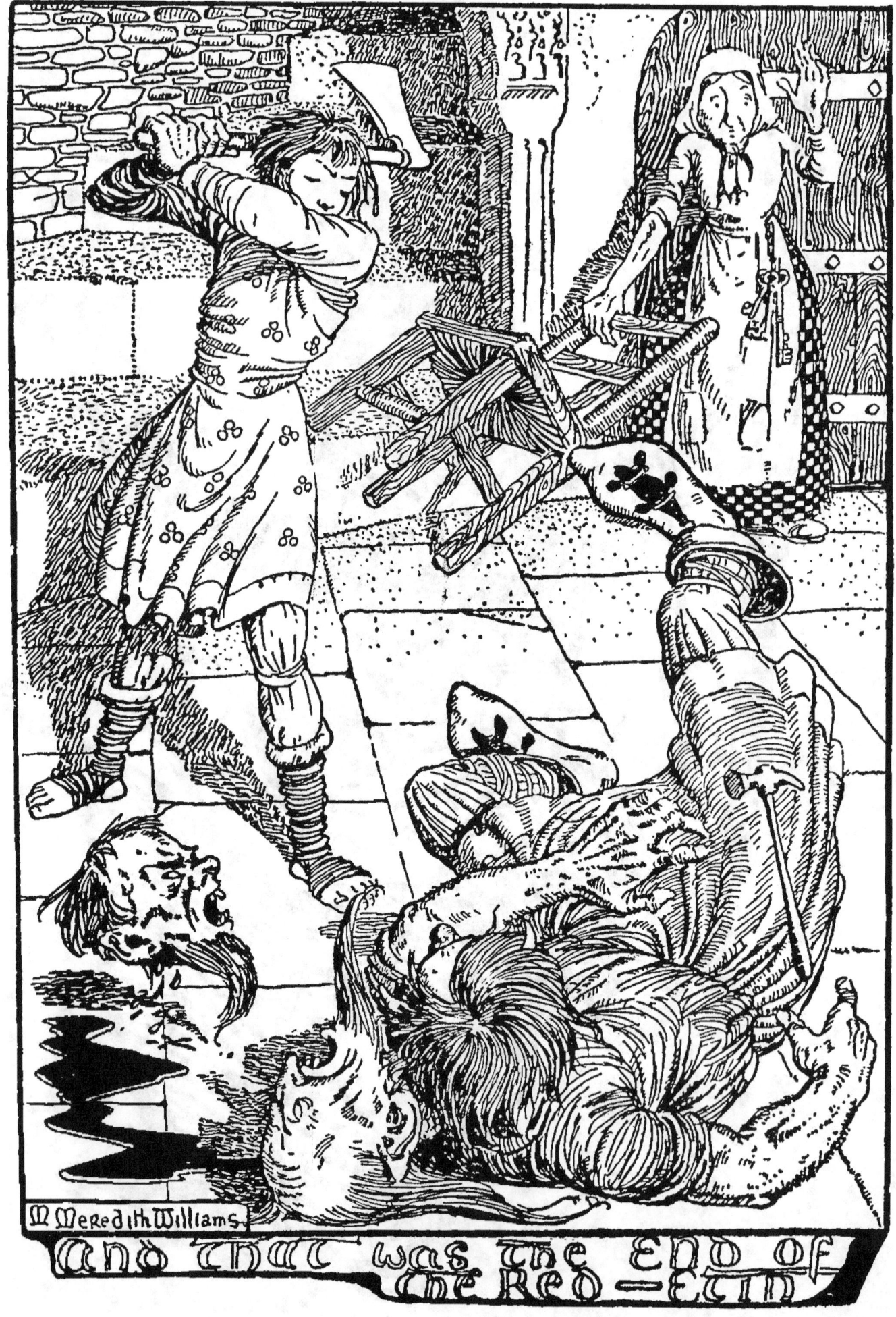

And that was the end of the Red-Etin

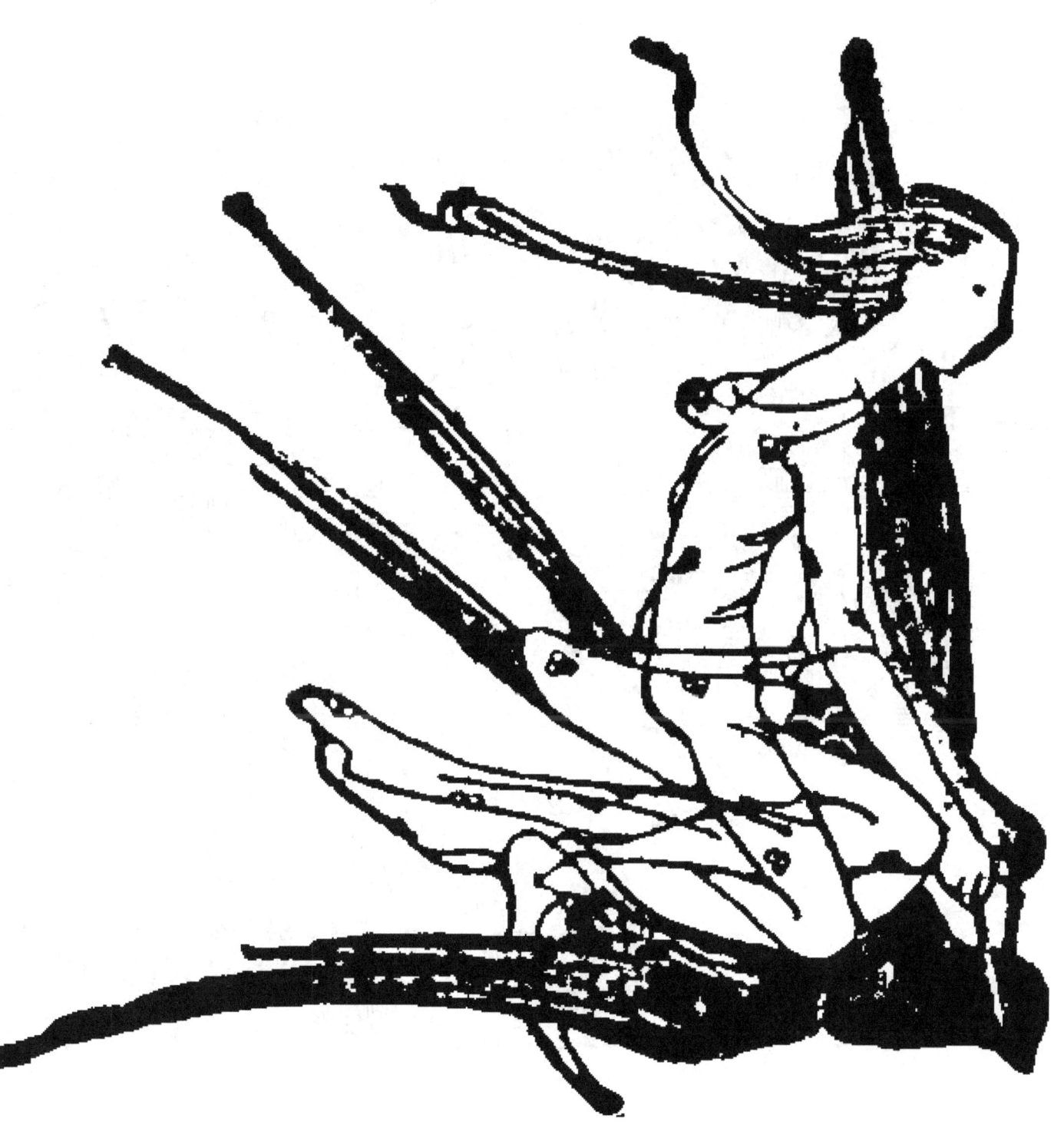

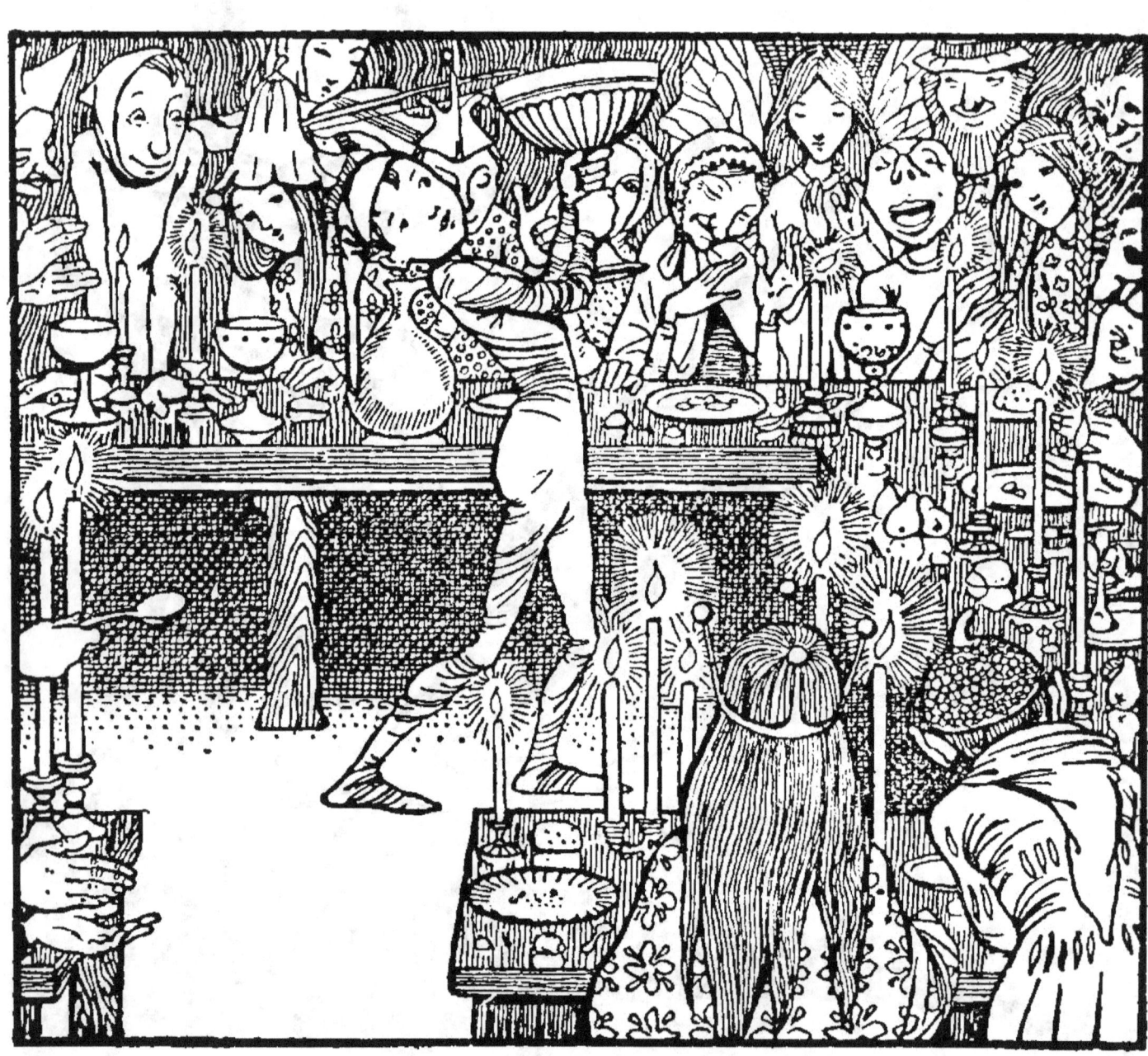

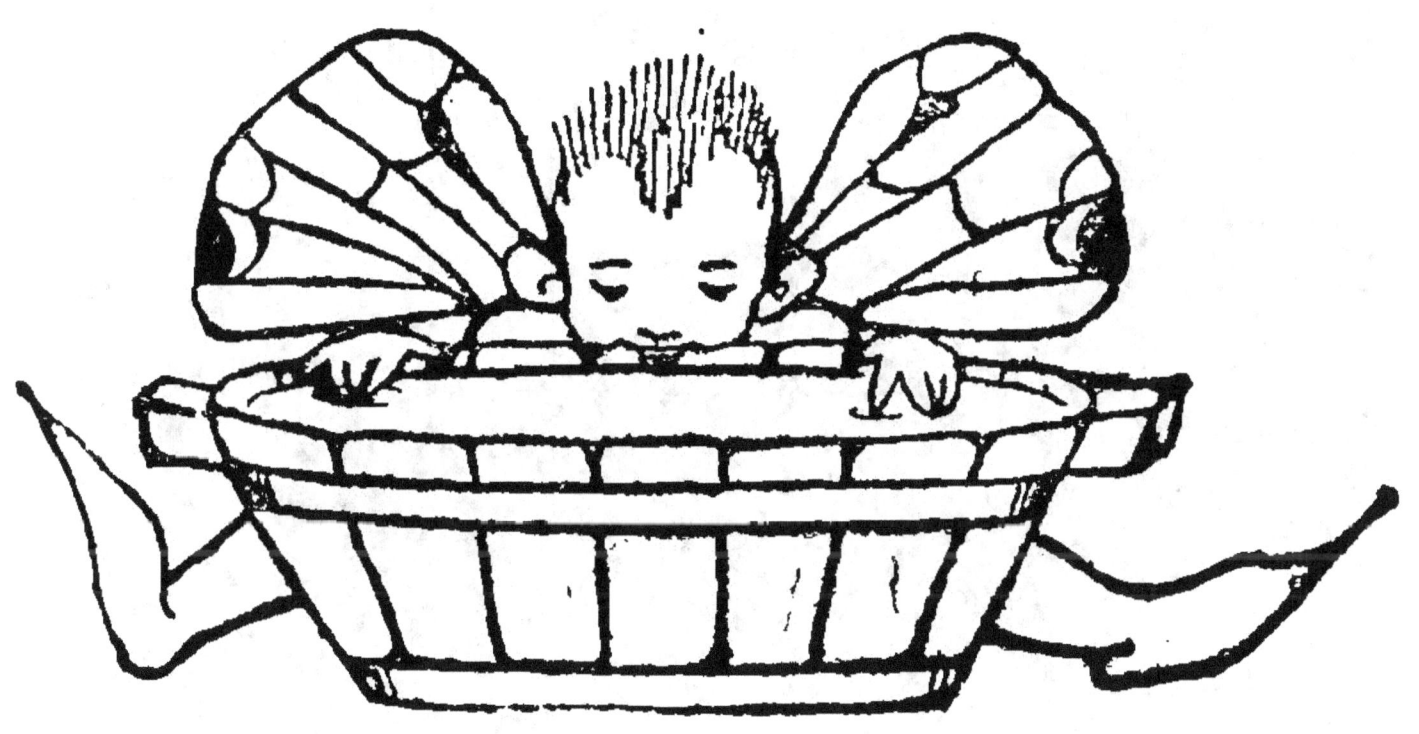

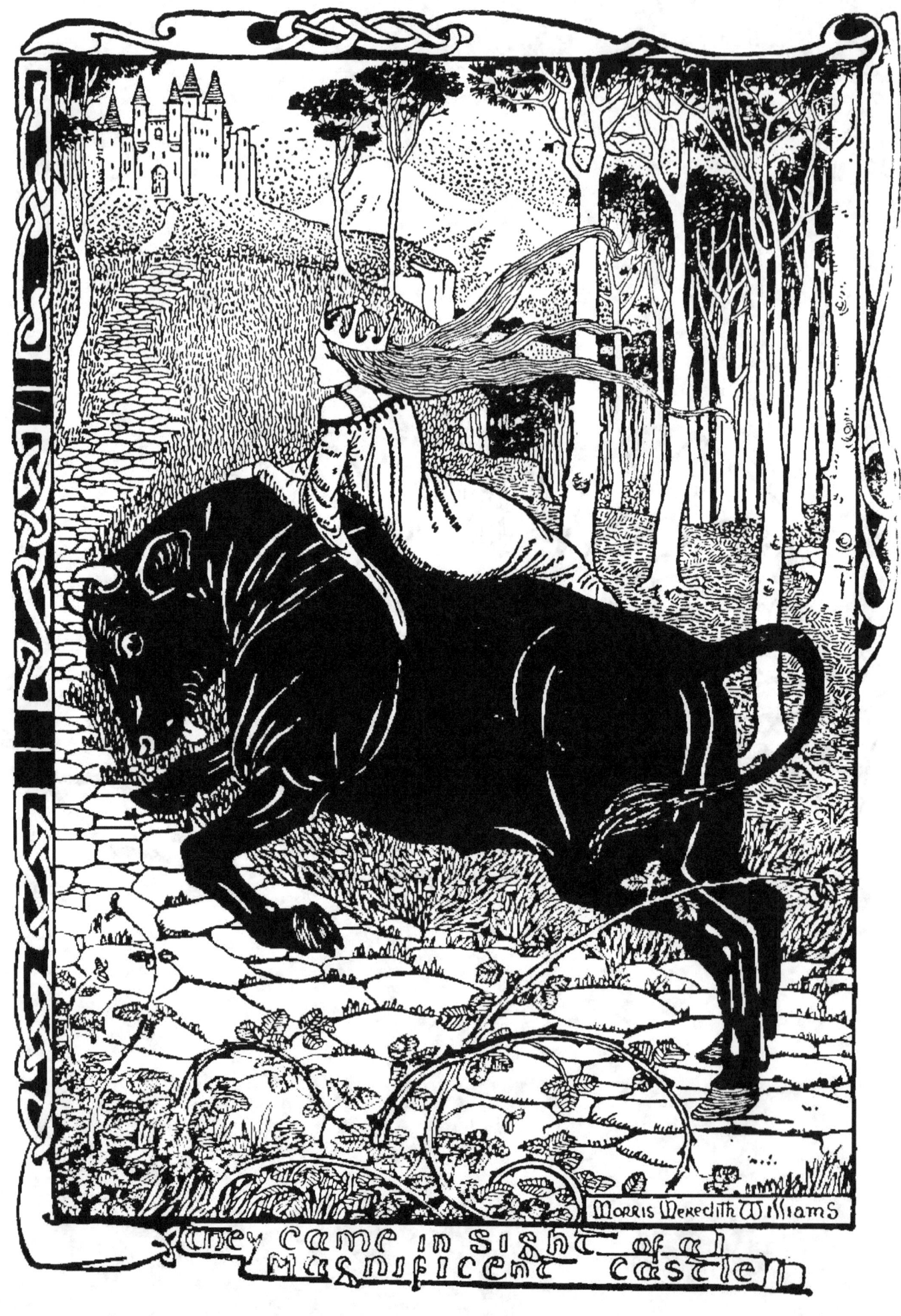

They came in sight of a magnificent castle

Morris Meredith Williams

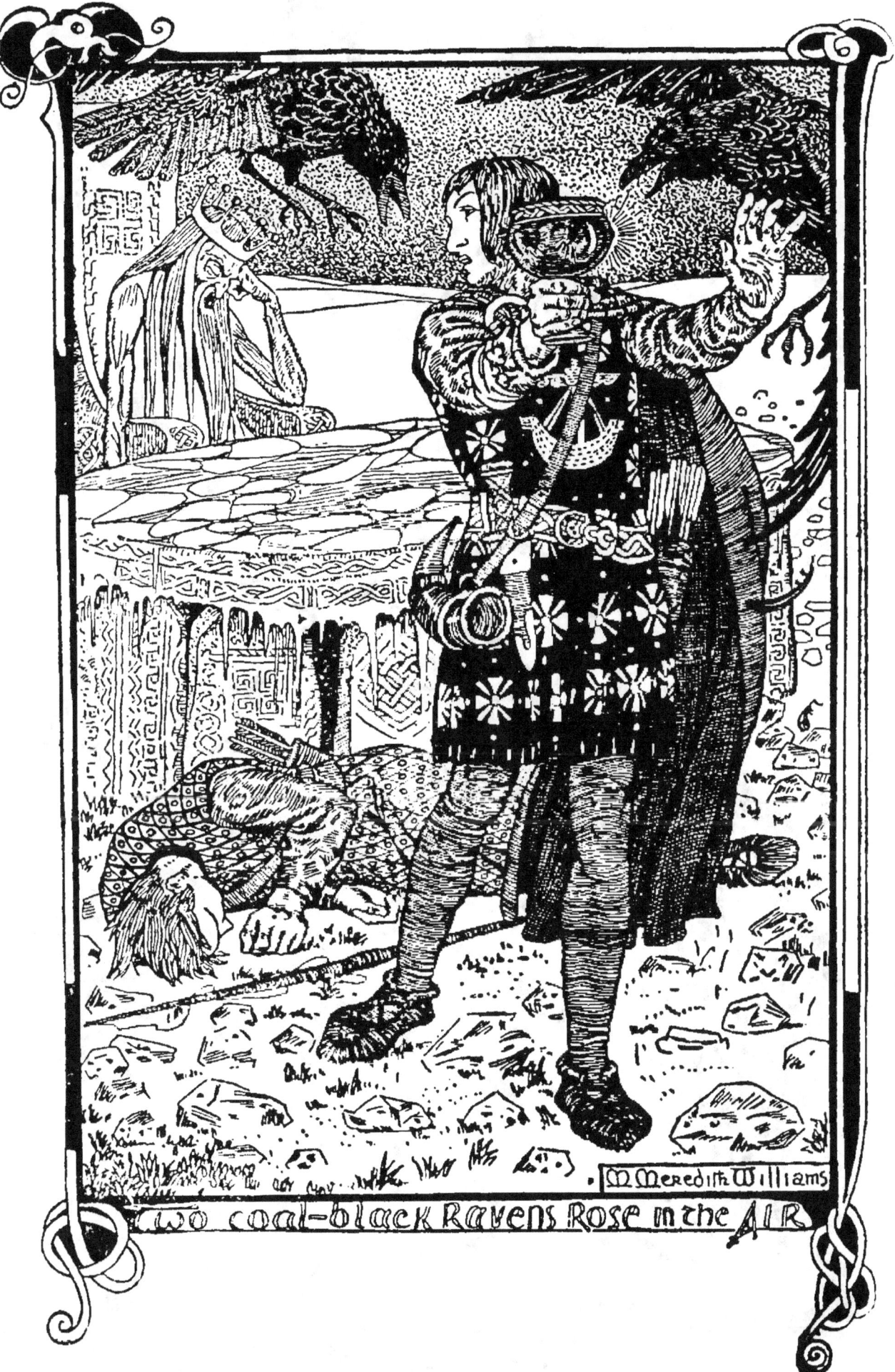

TWO COAL-BLACK RAVENS ROSE IN THE AIR

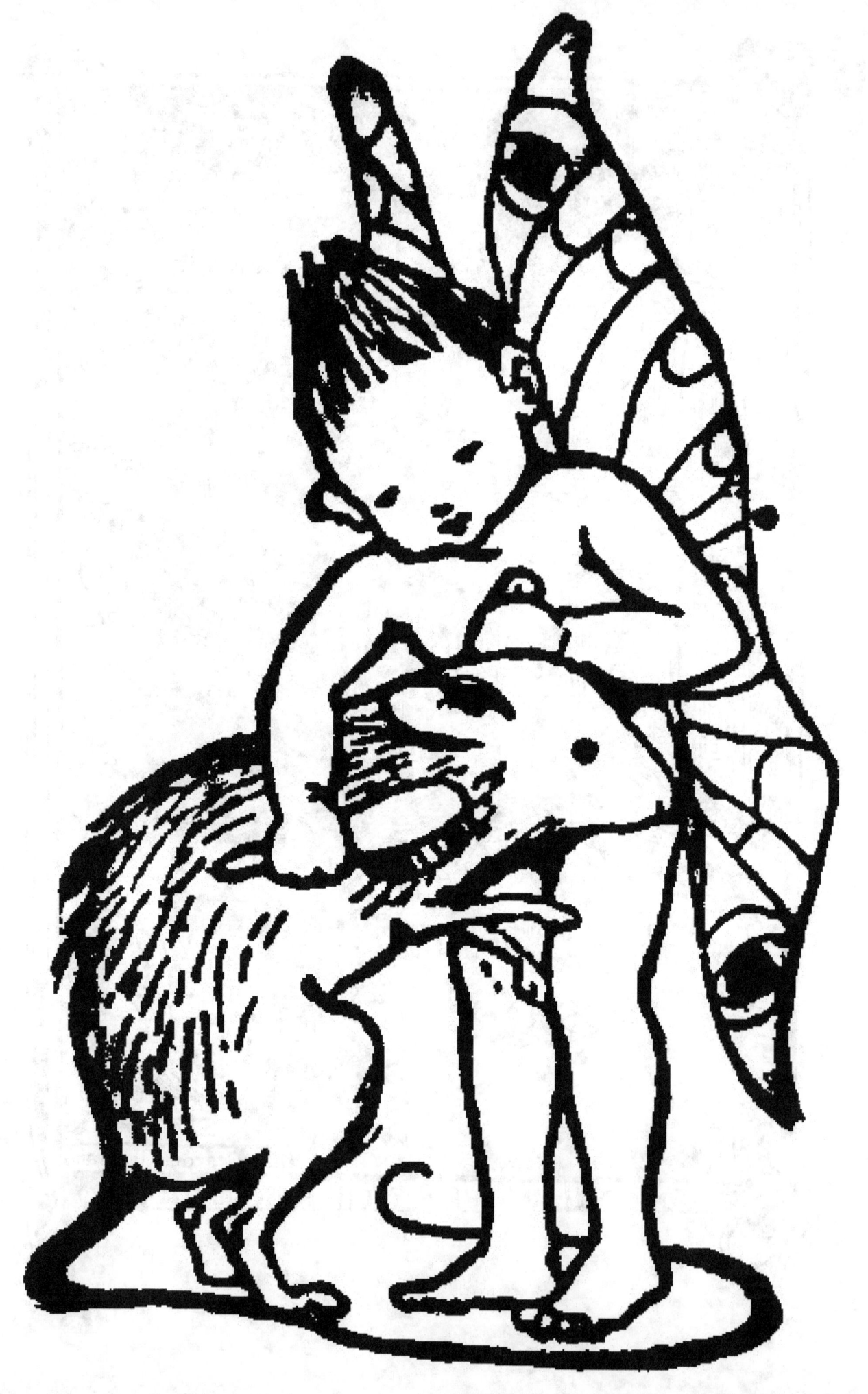

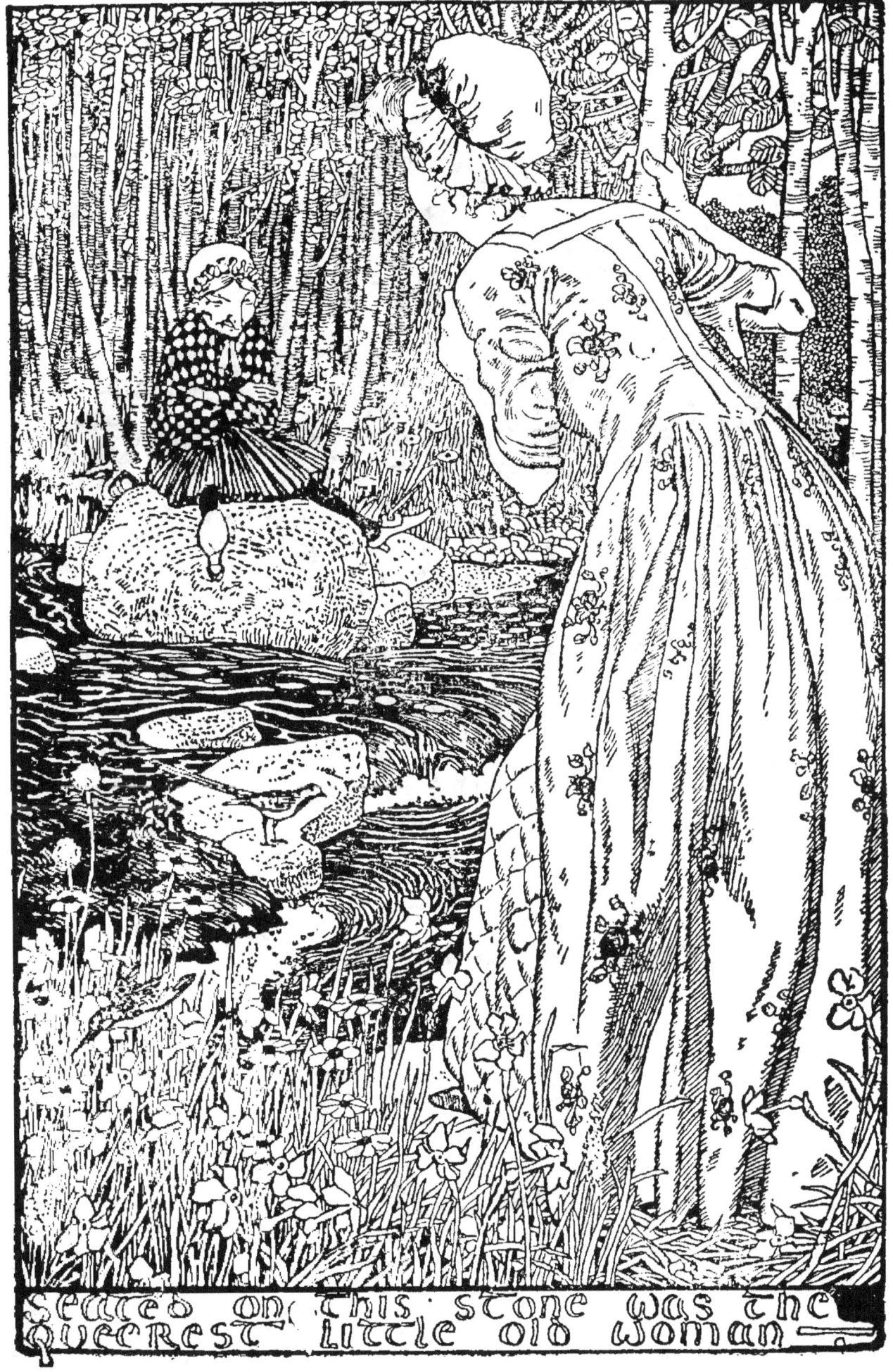

Seated on this stone was the queerest little old woman.

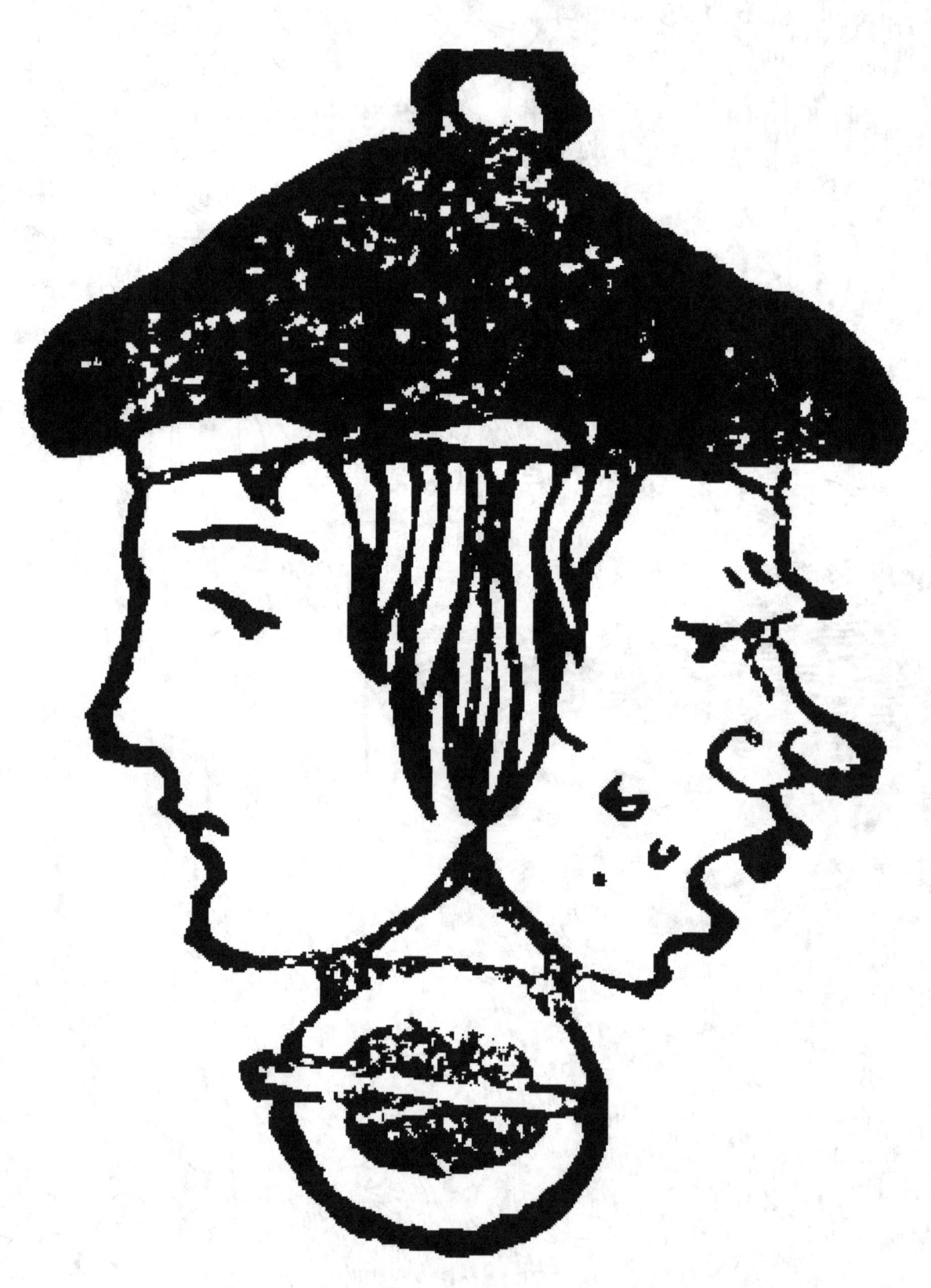

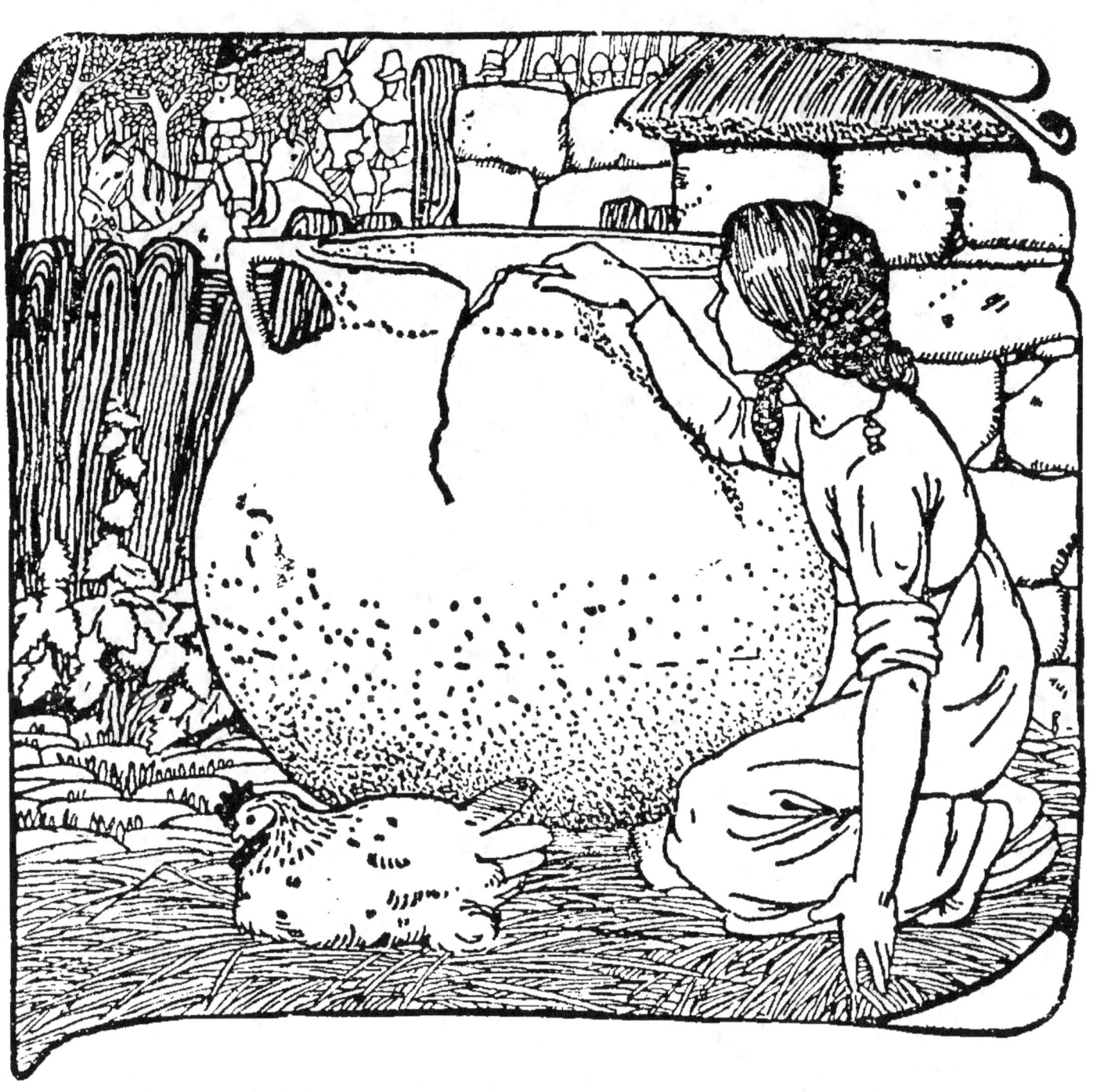

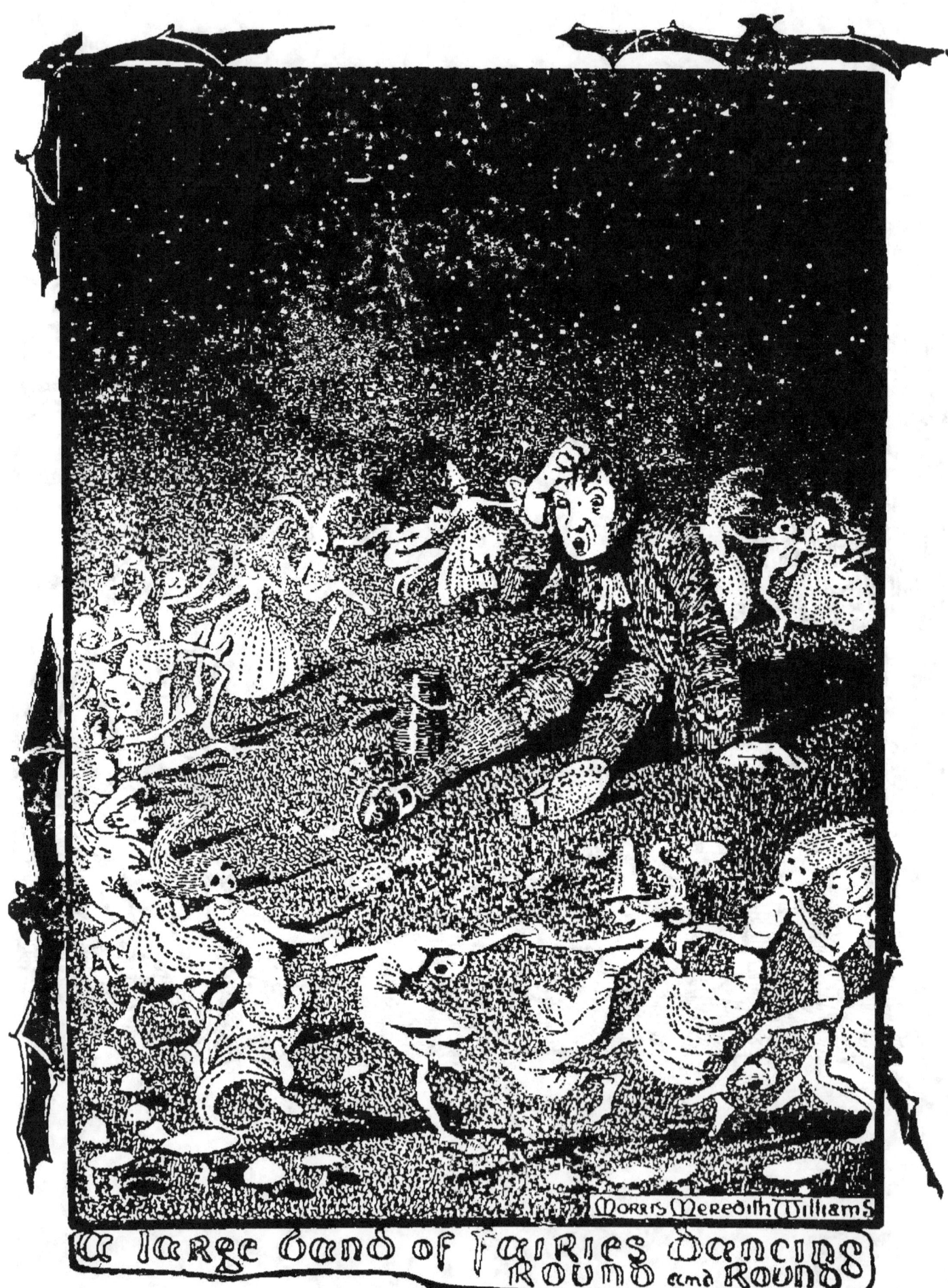

A large band of fairies dancing round and round

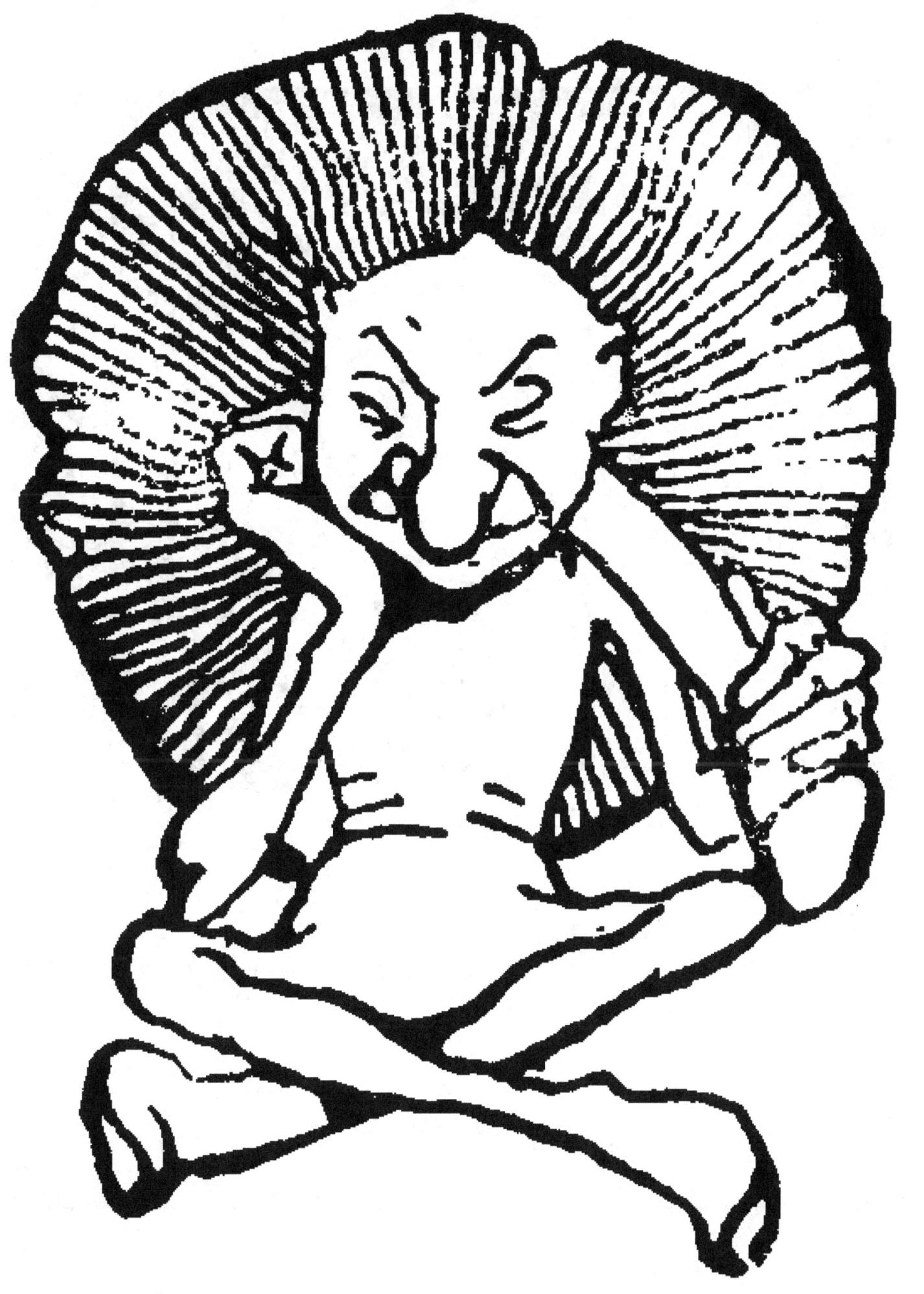

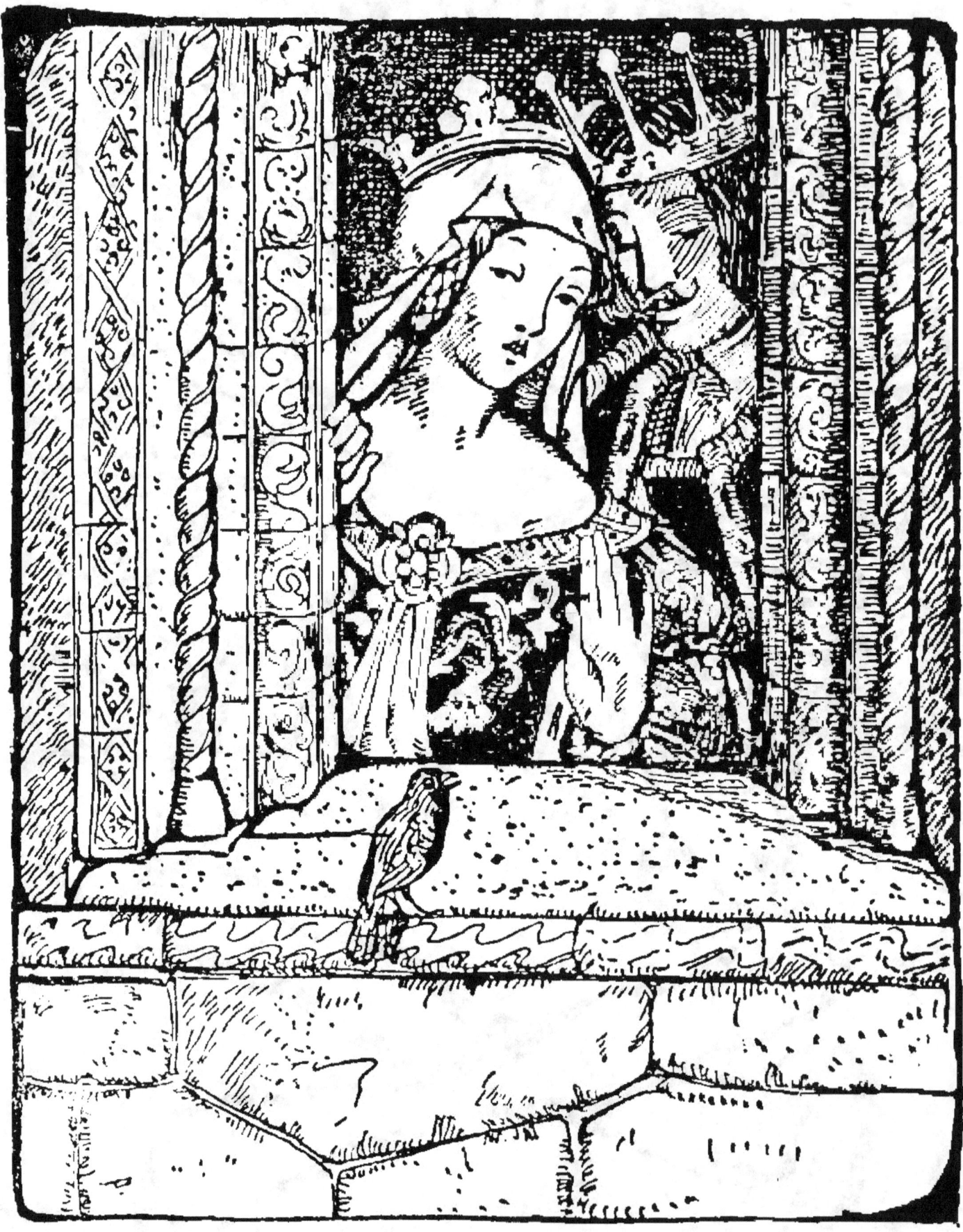

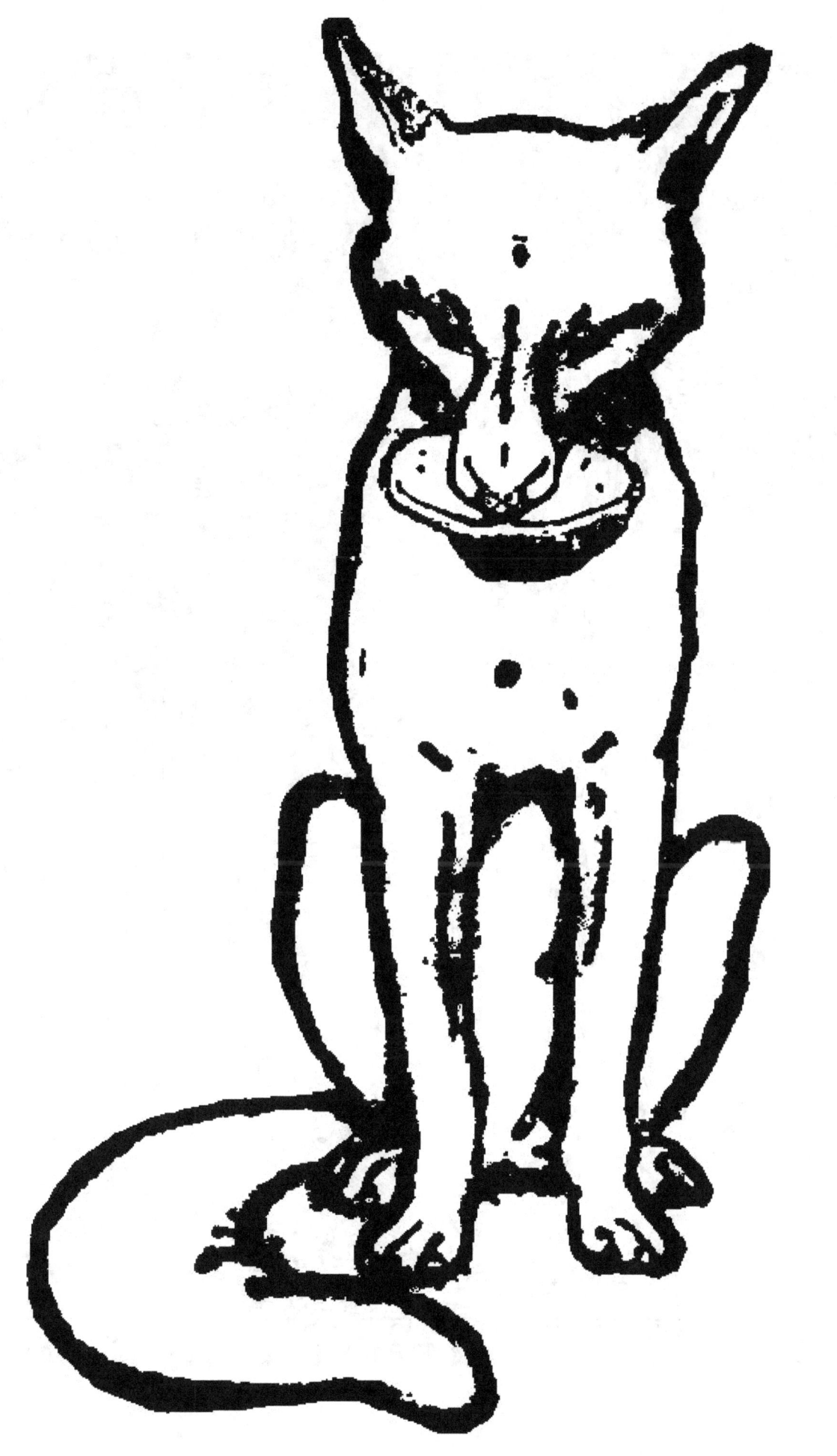

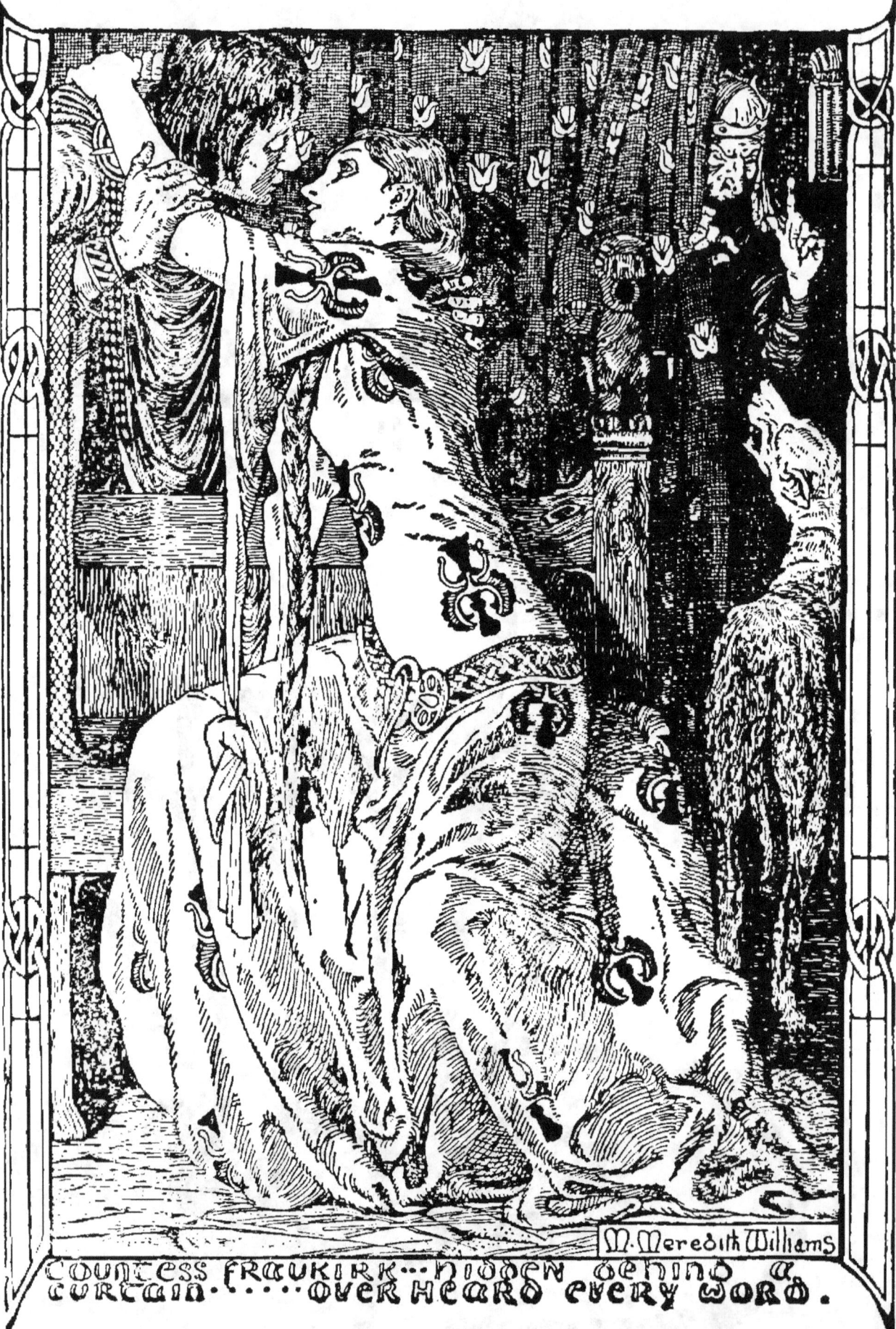

COUNTESS FRAUKIRK...HIDDEN BEHIND A
CURTAIN.....OVER HEARD EVERY WORD.

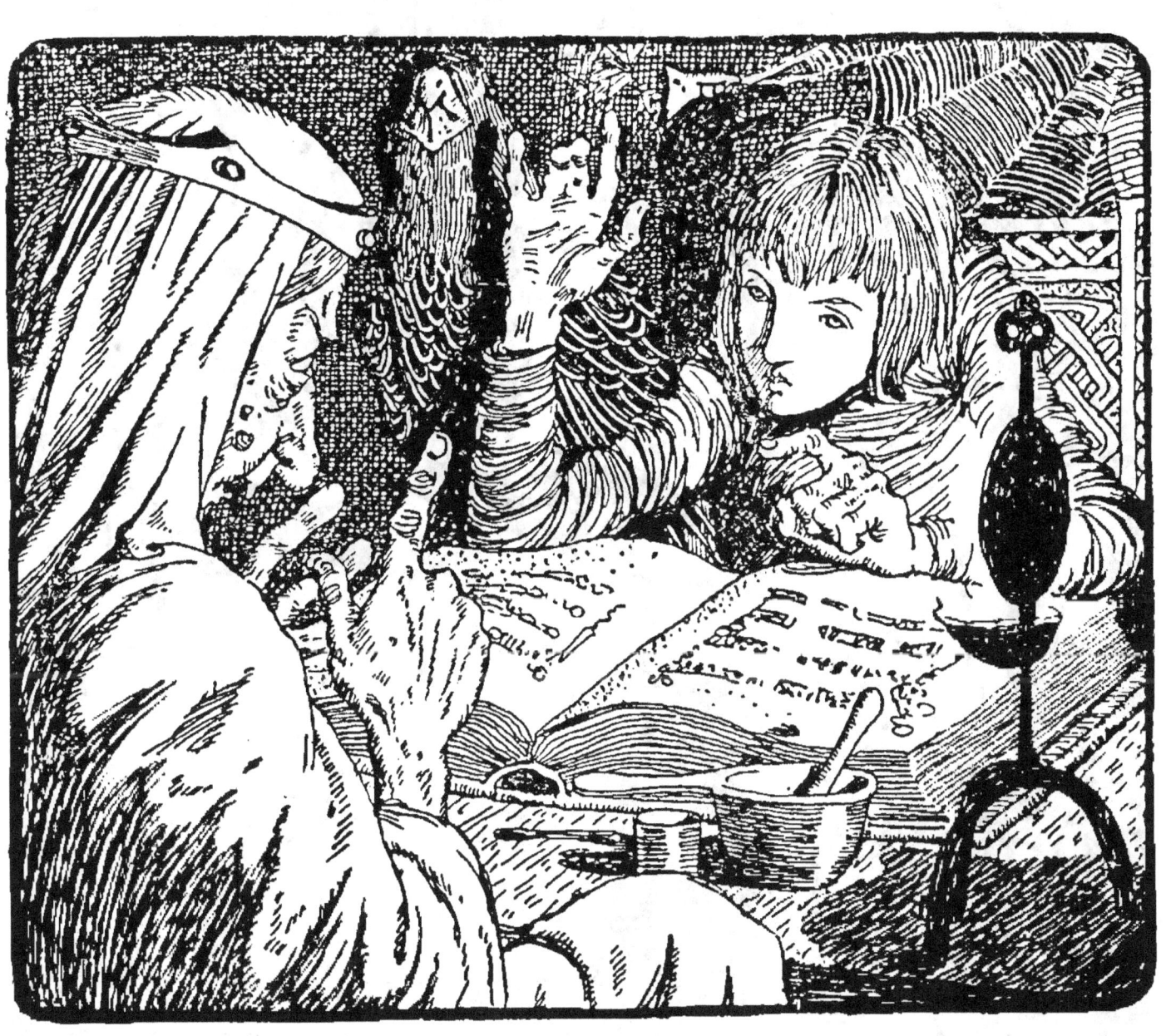

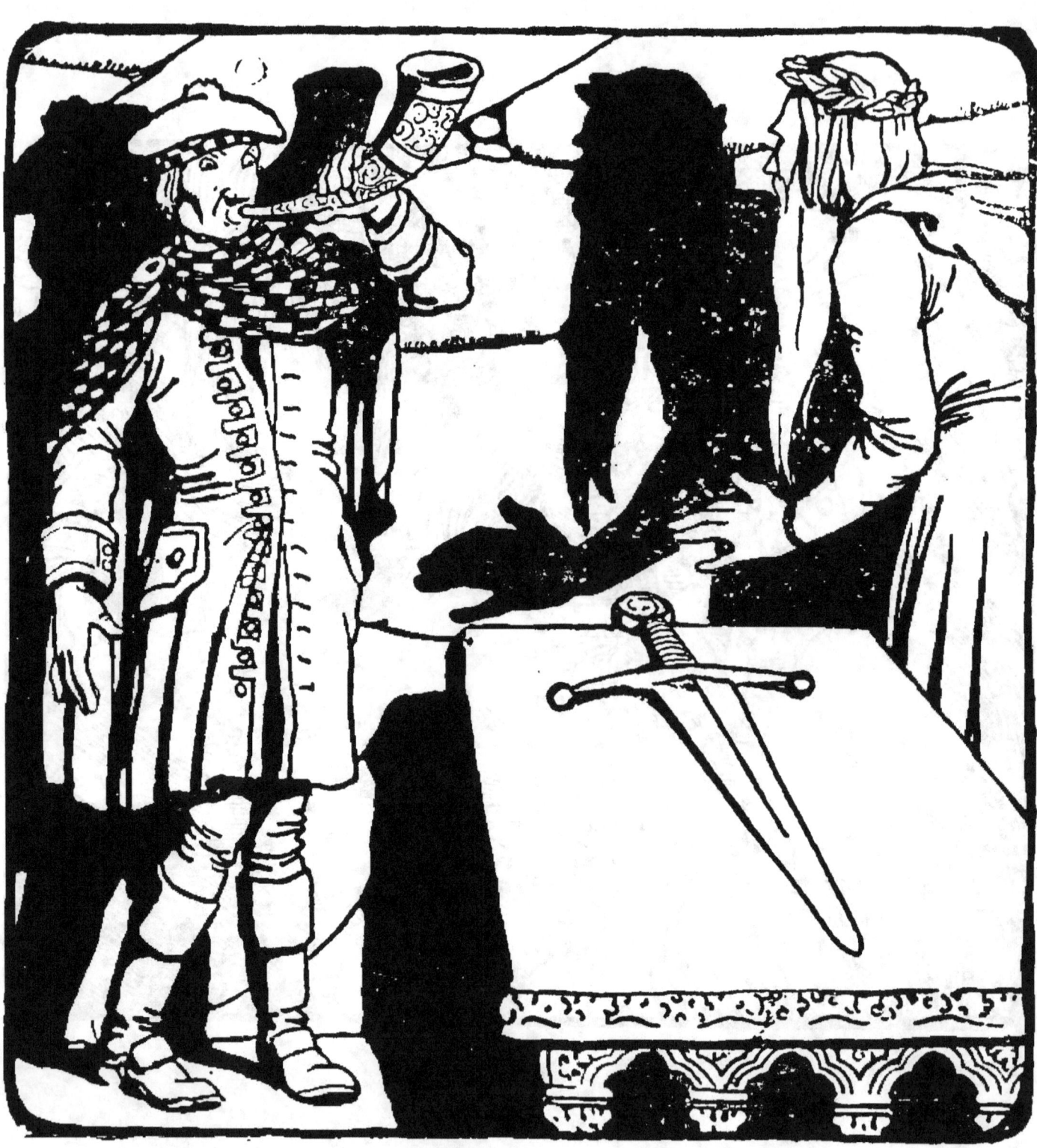

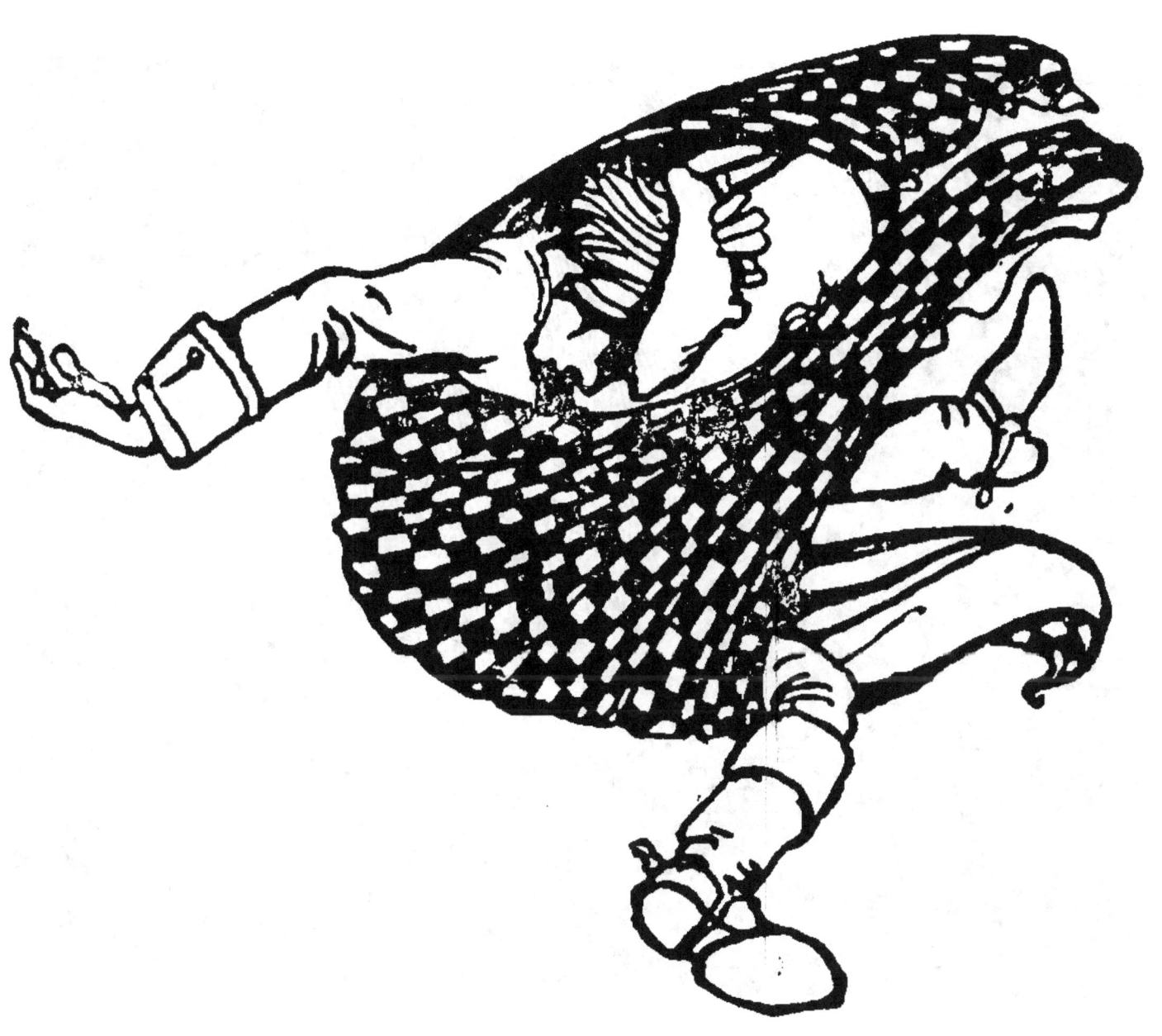

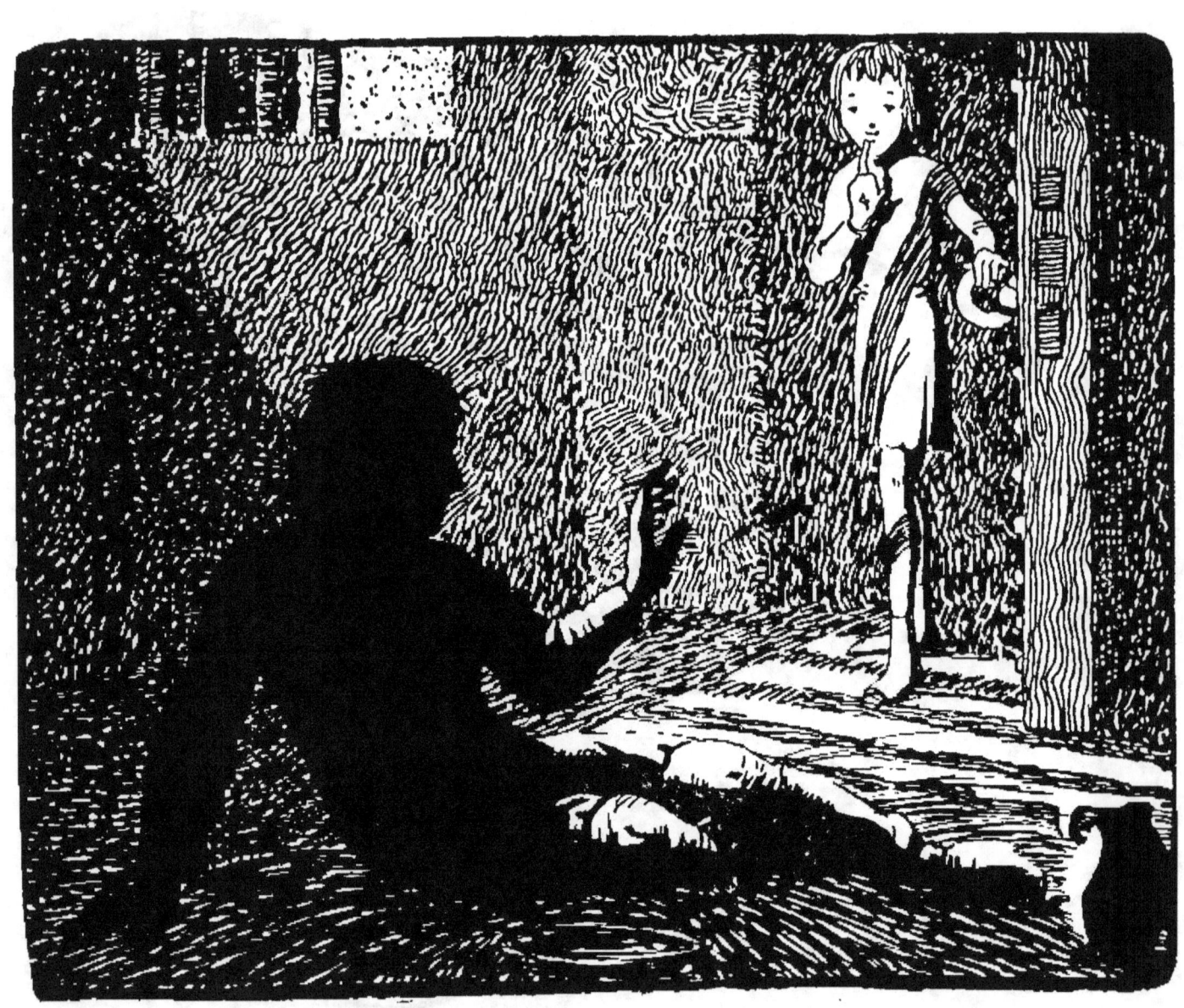

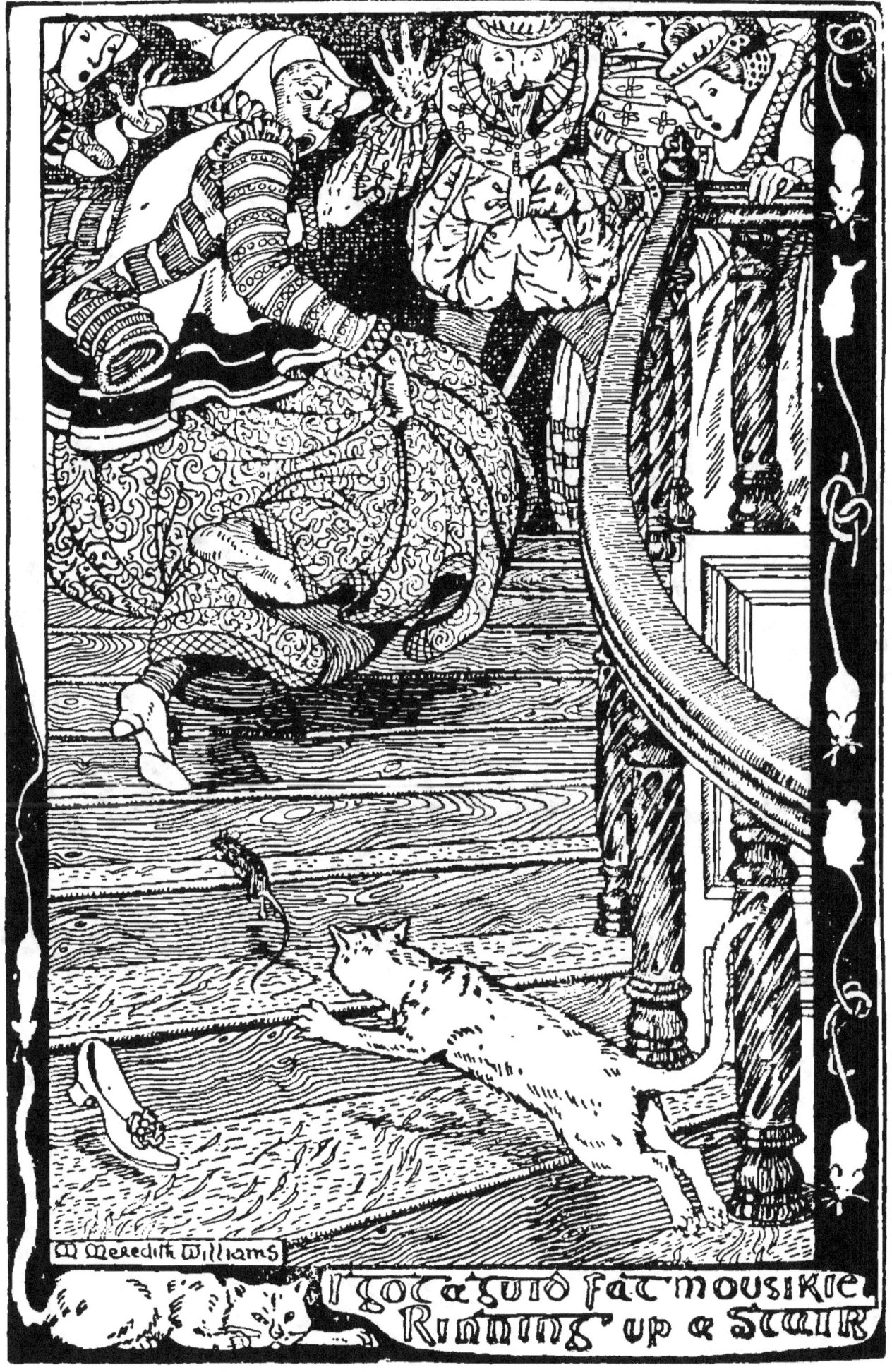

A Meredith Williams

I got a guid fat mousikie
Rinning up a stair

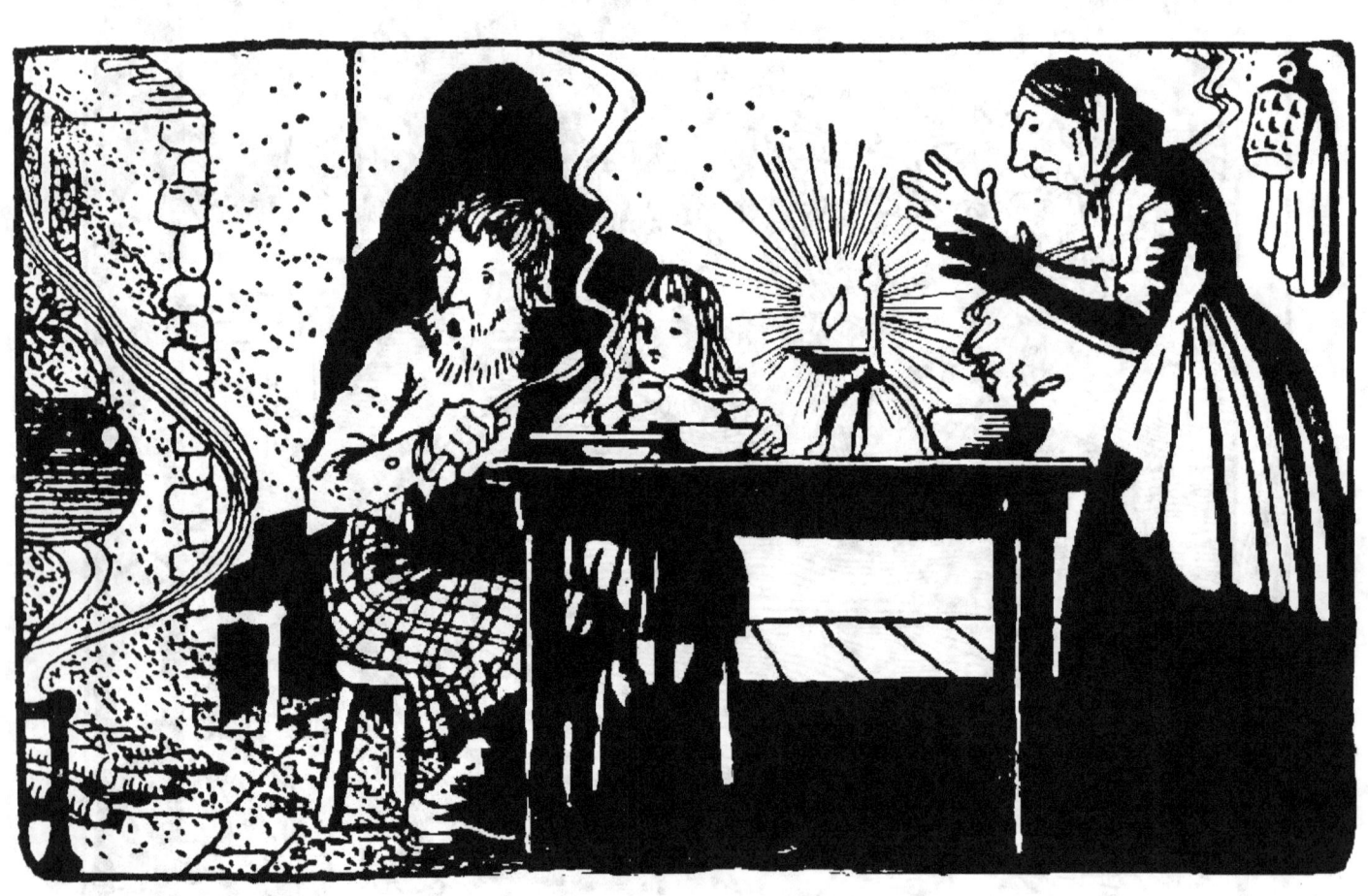

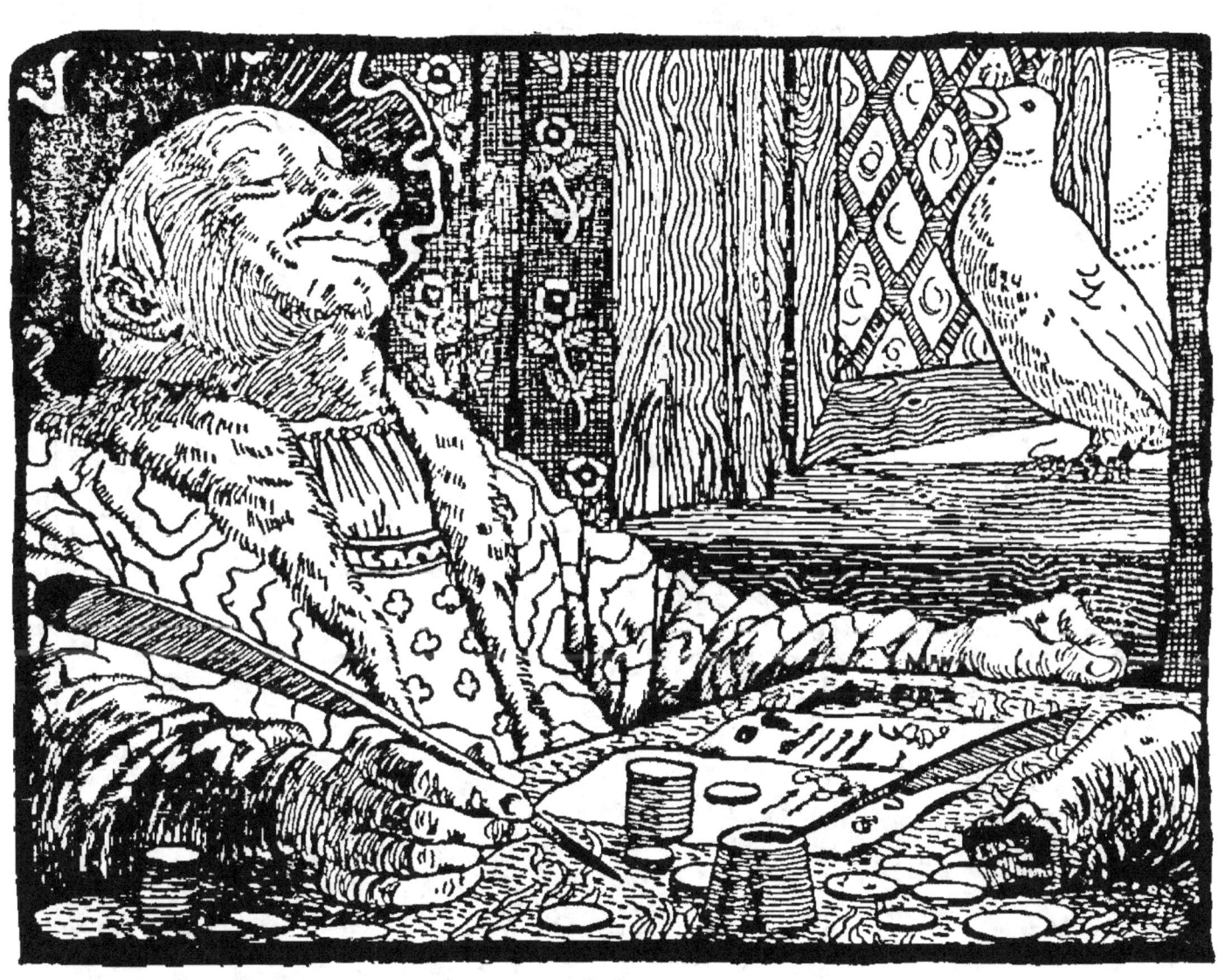

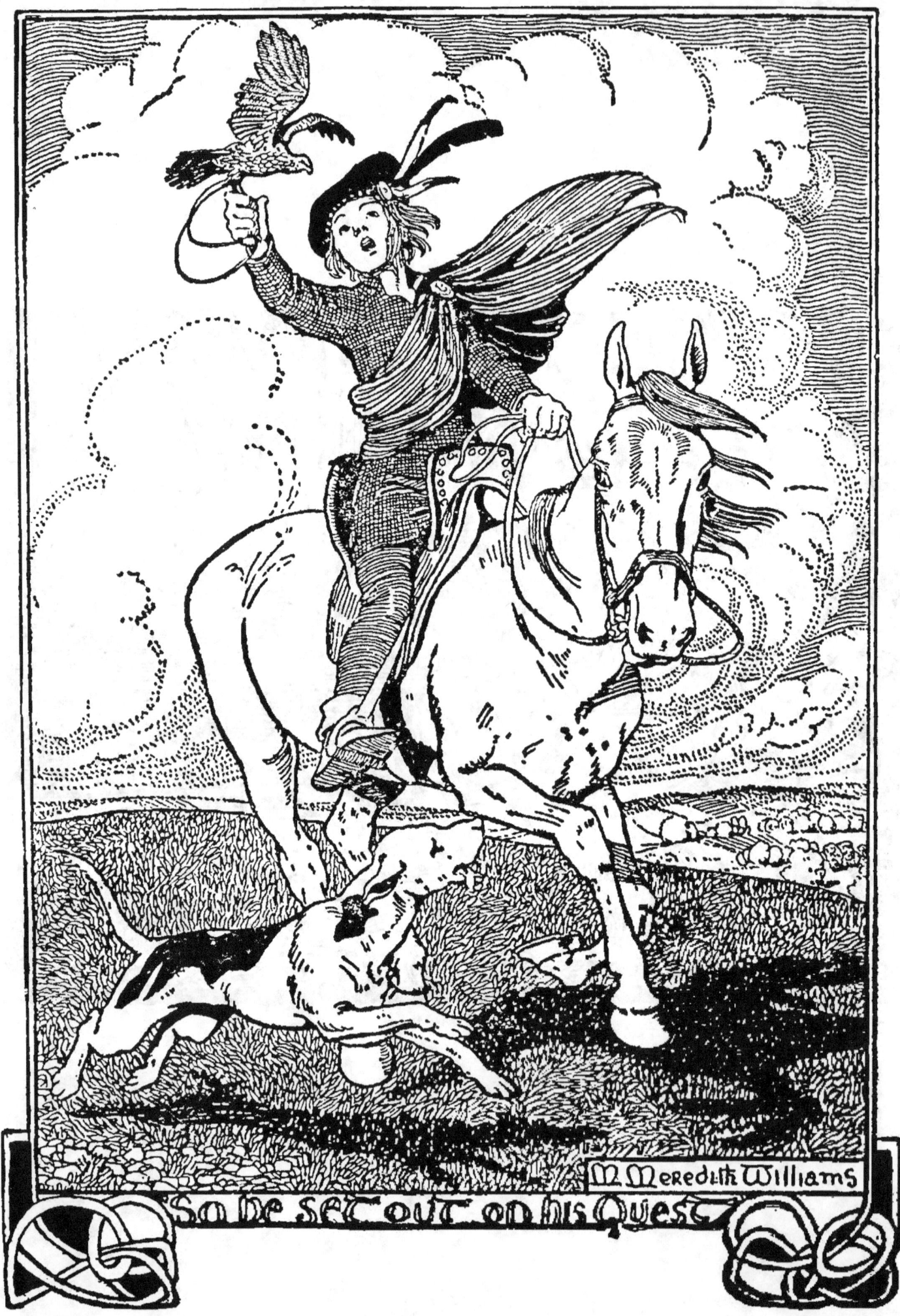

So he set out on his Quest

M. Meredith Williams

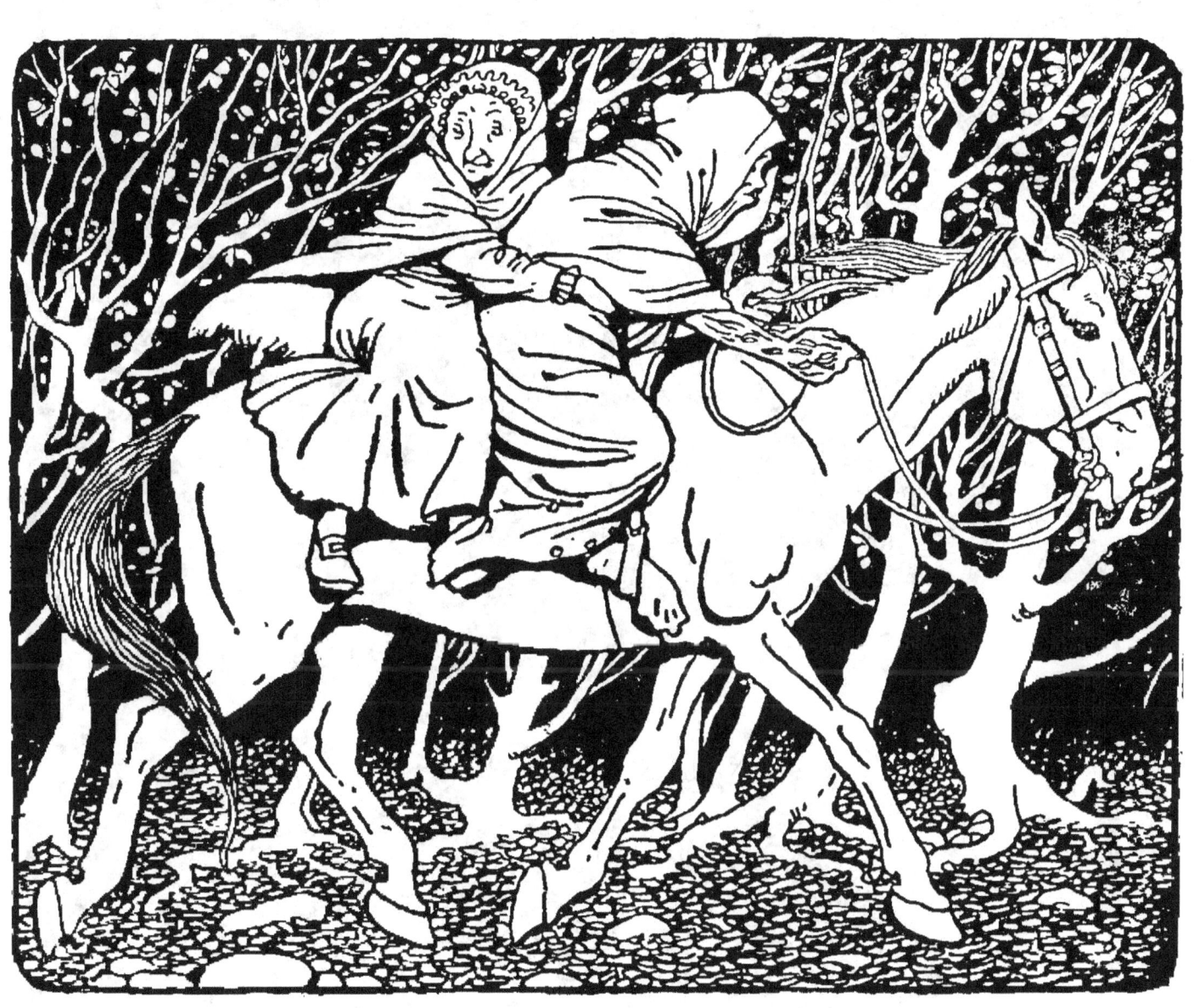

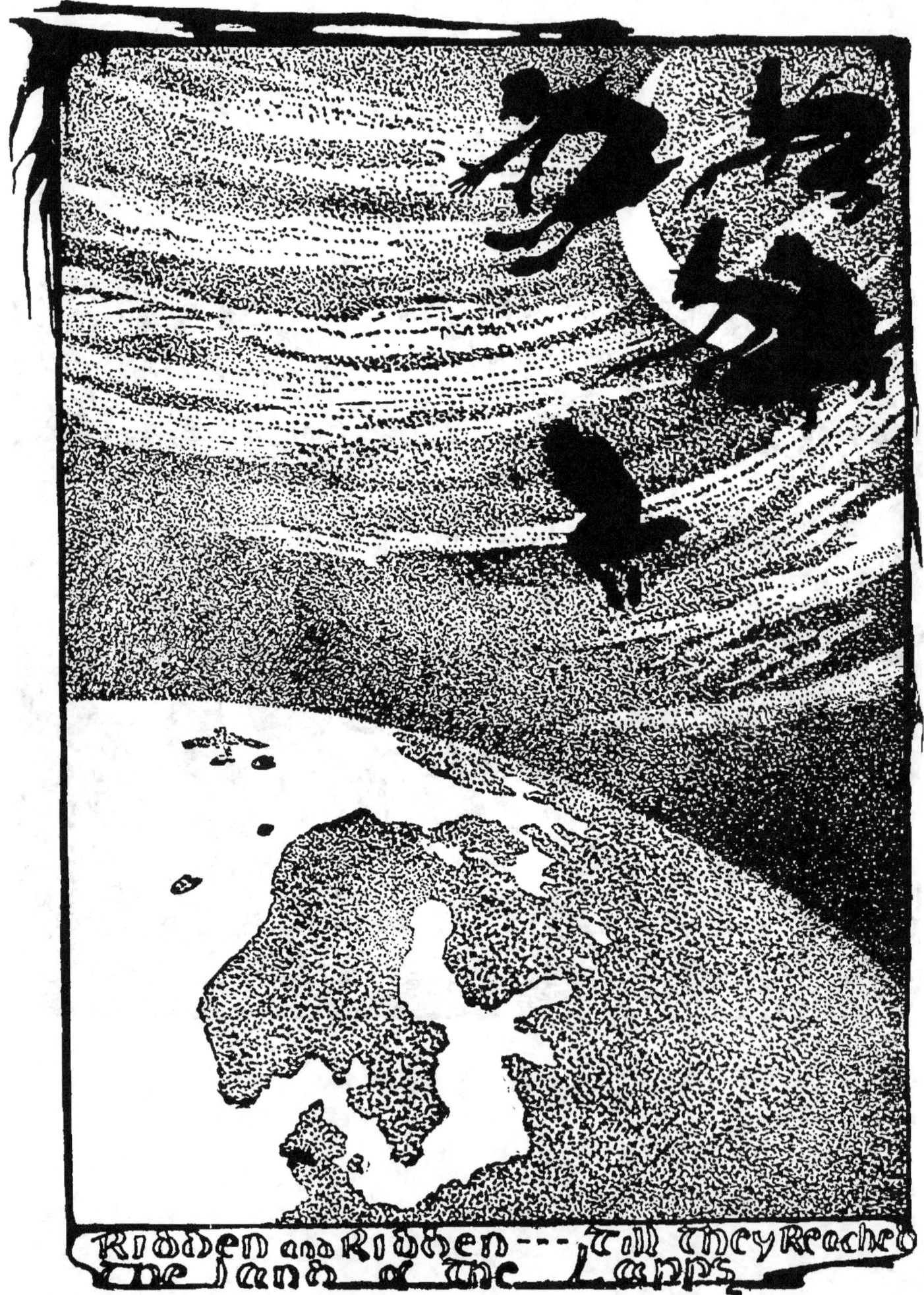

Ridden and Ridden --- Till They Reached the Land of the Lapps

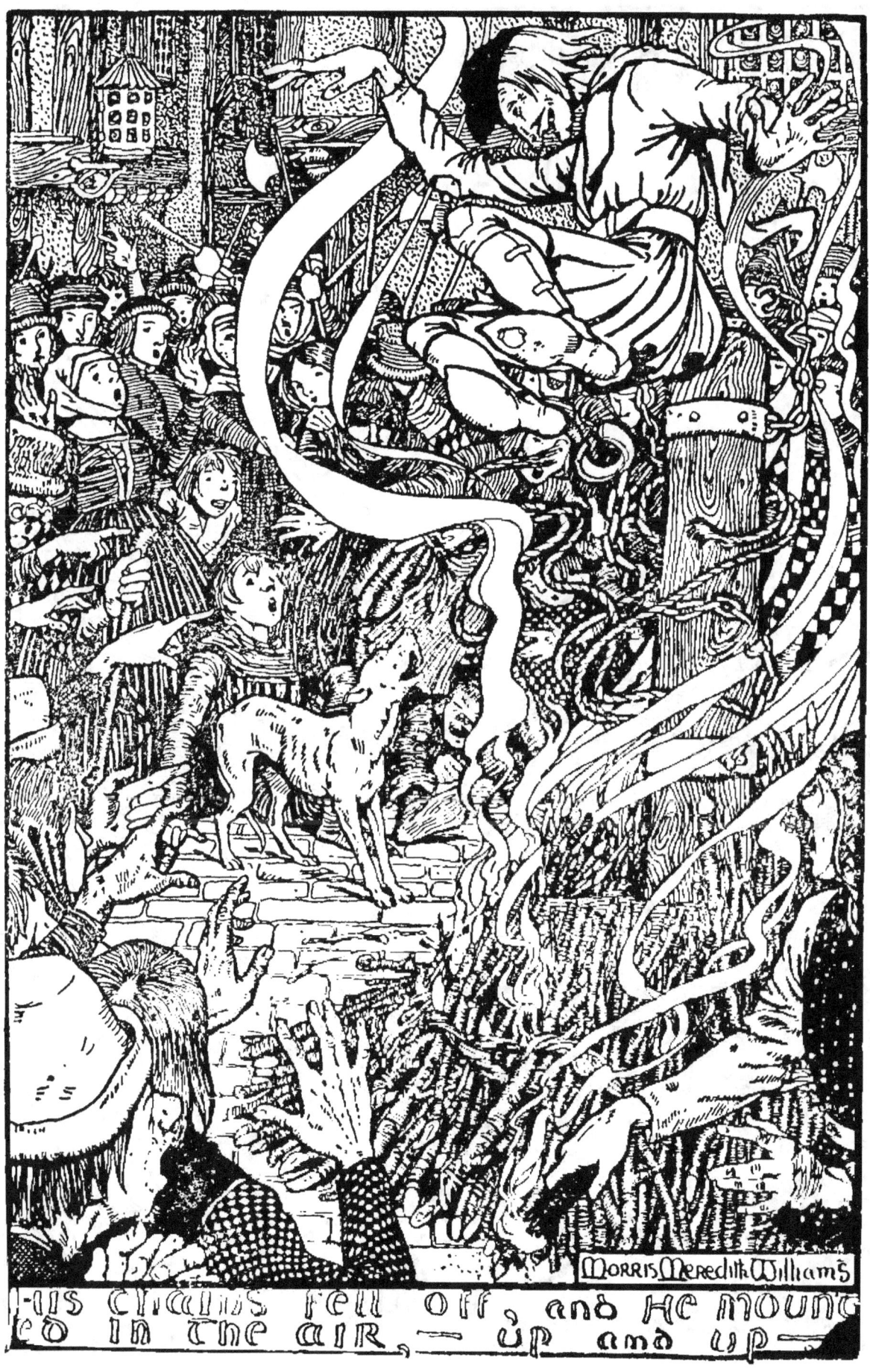

HIS CHAINS FELL OFF, AND HE MOUNTED IN THE AIR, — UP AND UP —

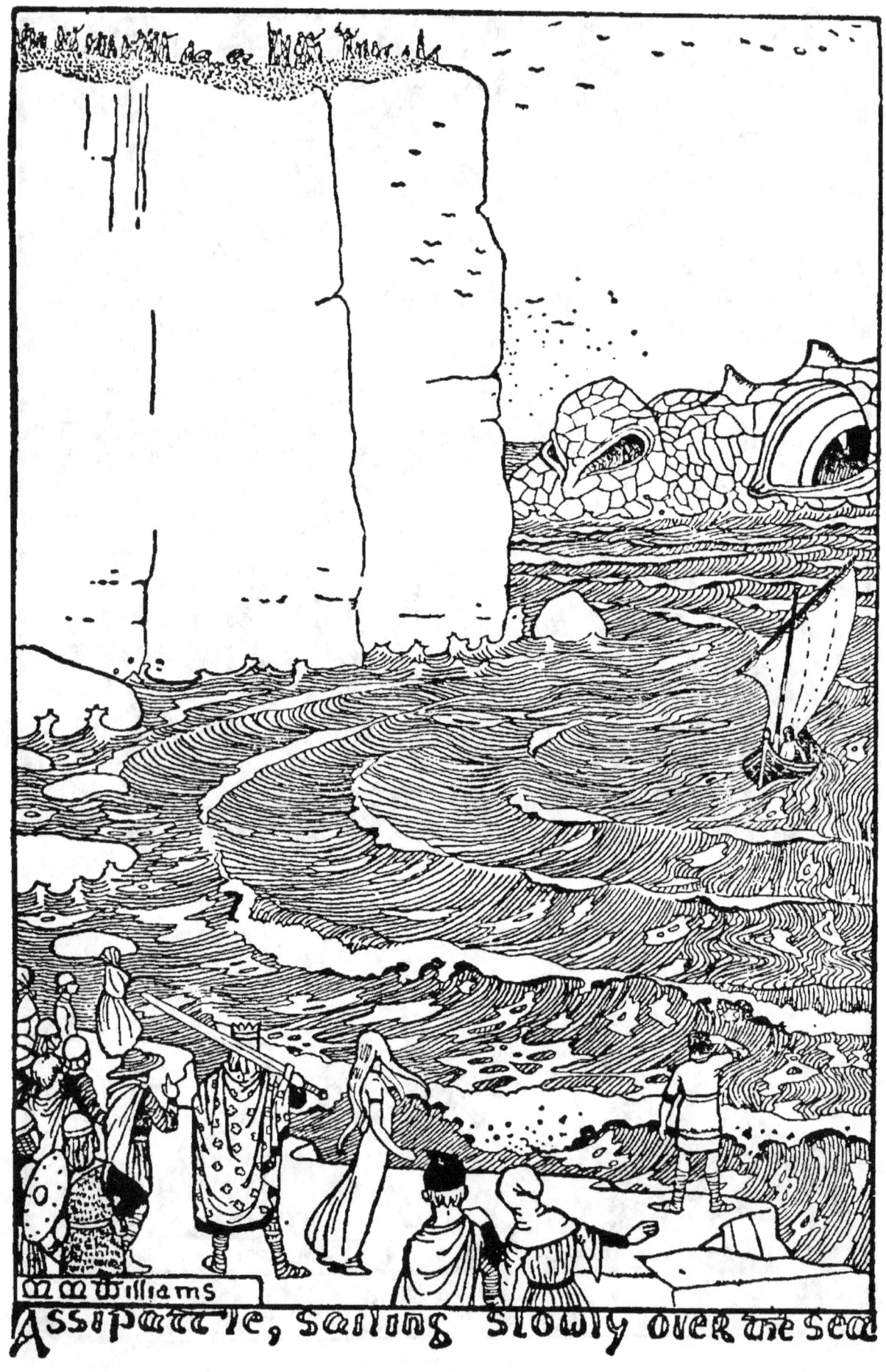

Assipattle, sailing slowly over the sea

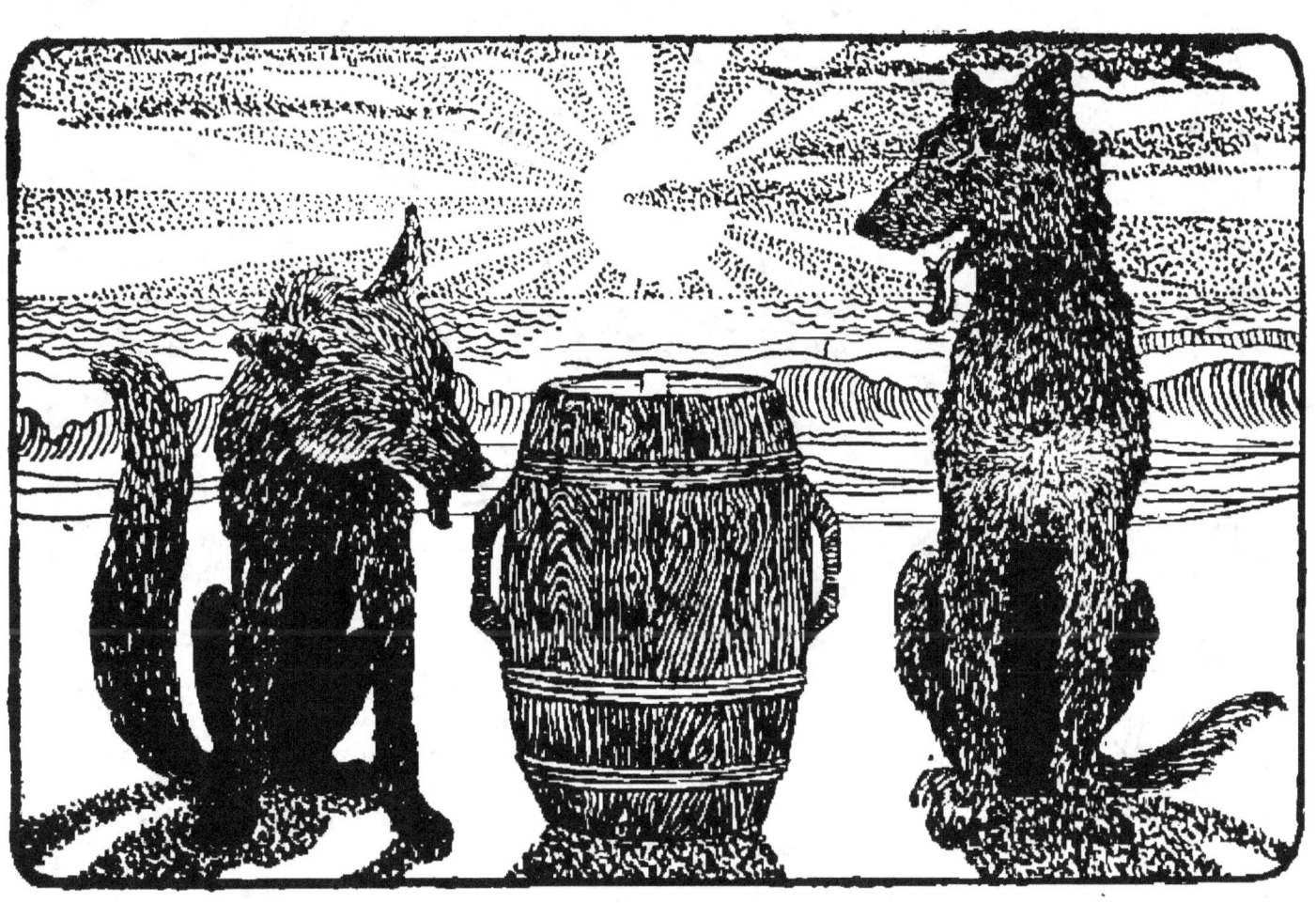

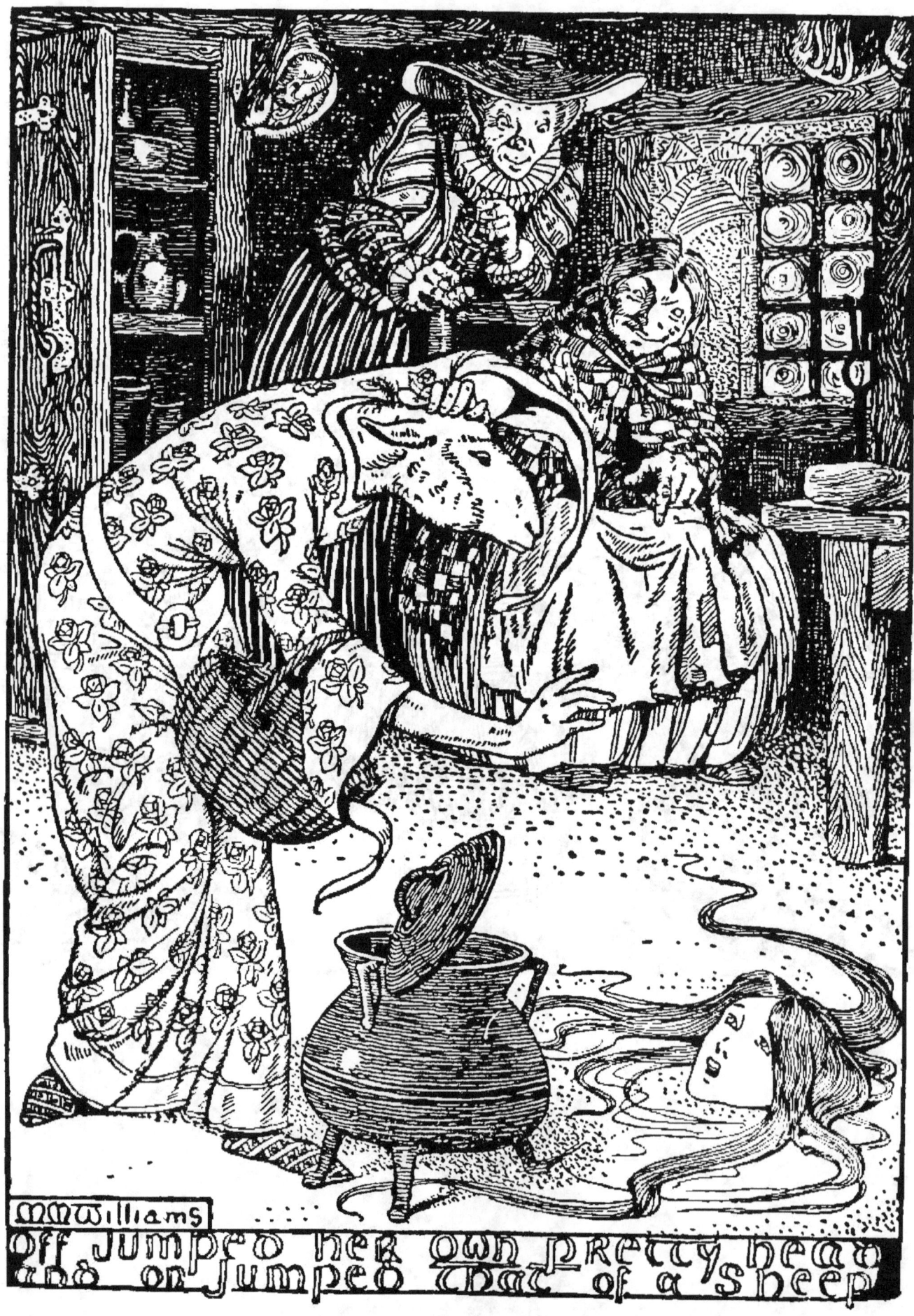

off jumped her own pretty head
and on jumped that of a sheep

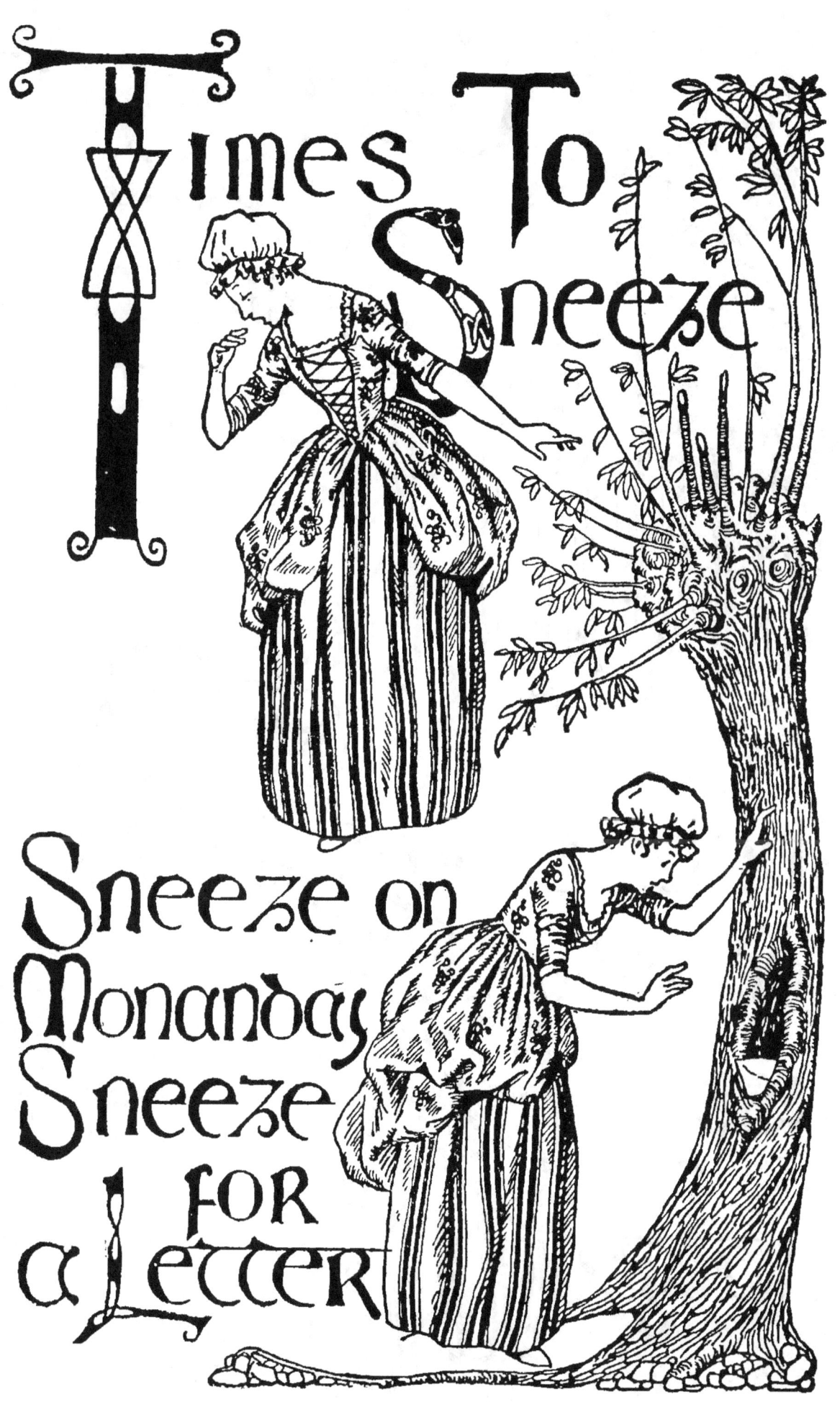

Times To Sneeze

Sneeze on
Monanday
Sneeze
for
a Letter

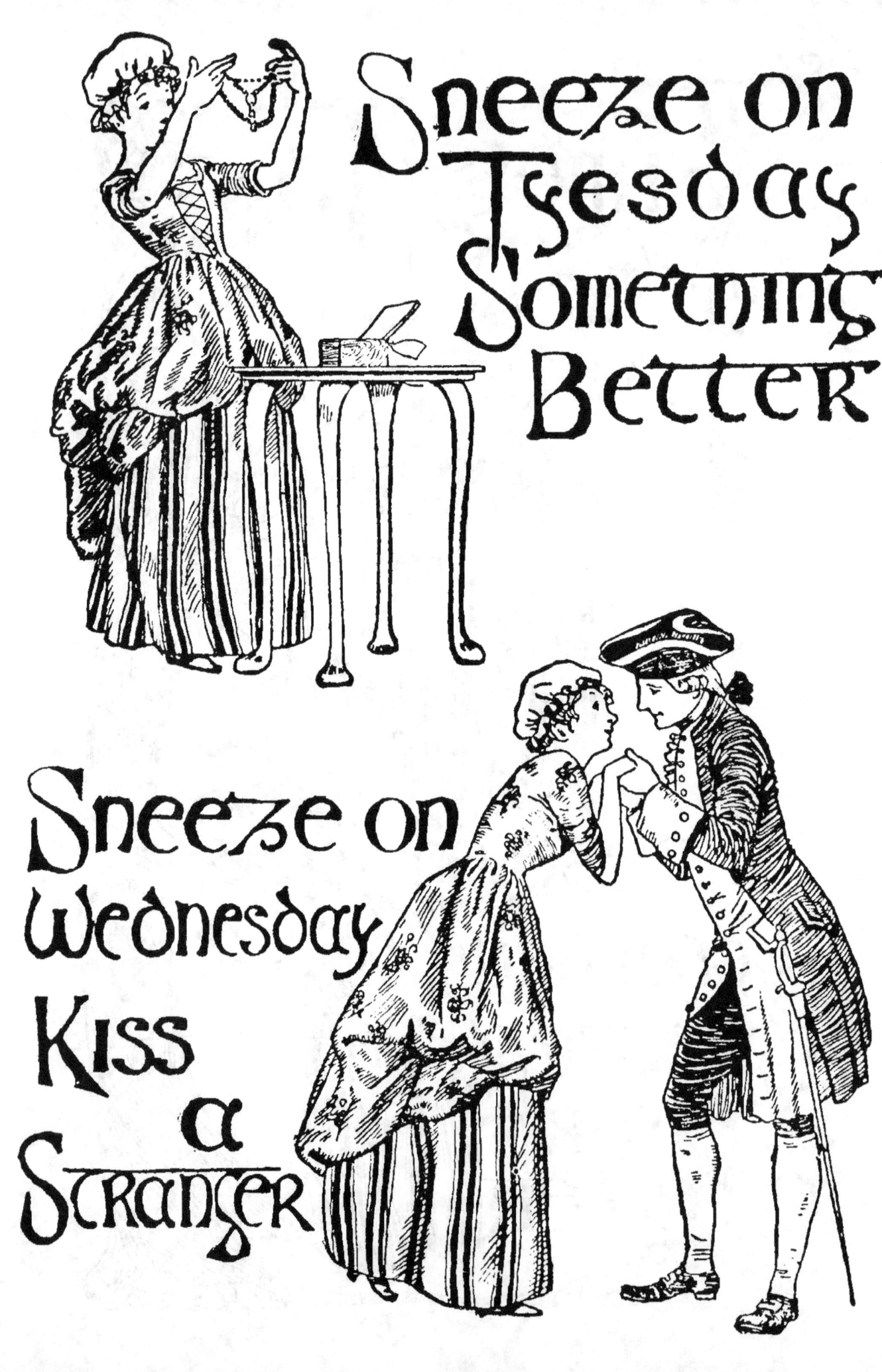

Sneeze on Tuesday
Something Better

Sneeze on Wednesday
Kiss a Stranger

Sneeze on Teersday Sneeze for Danger

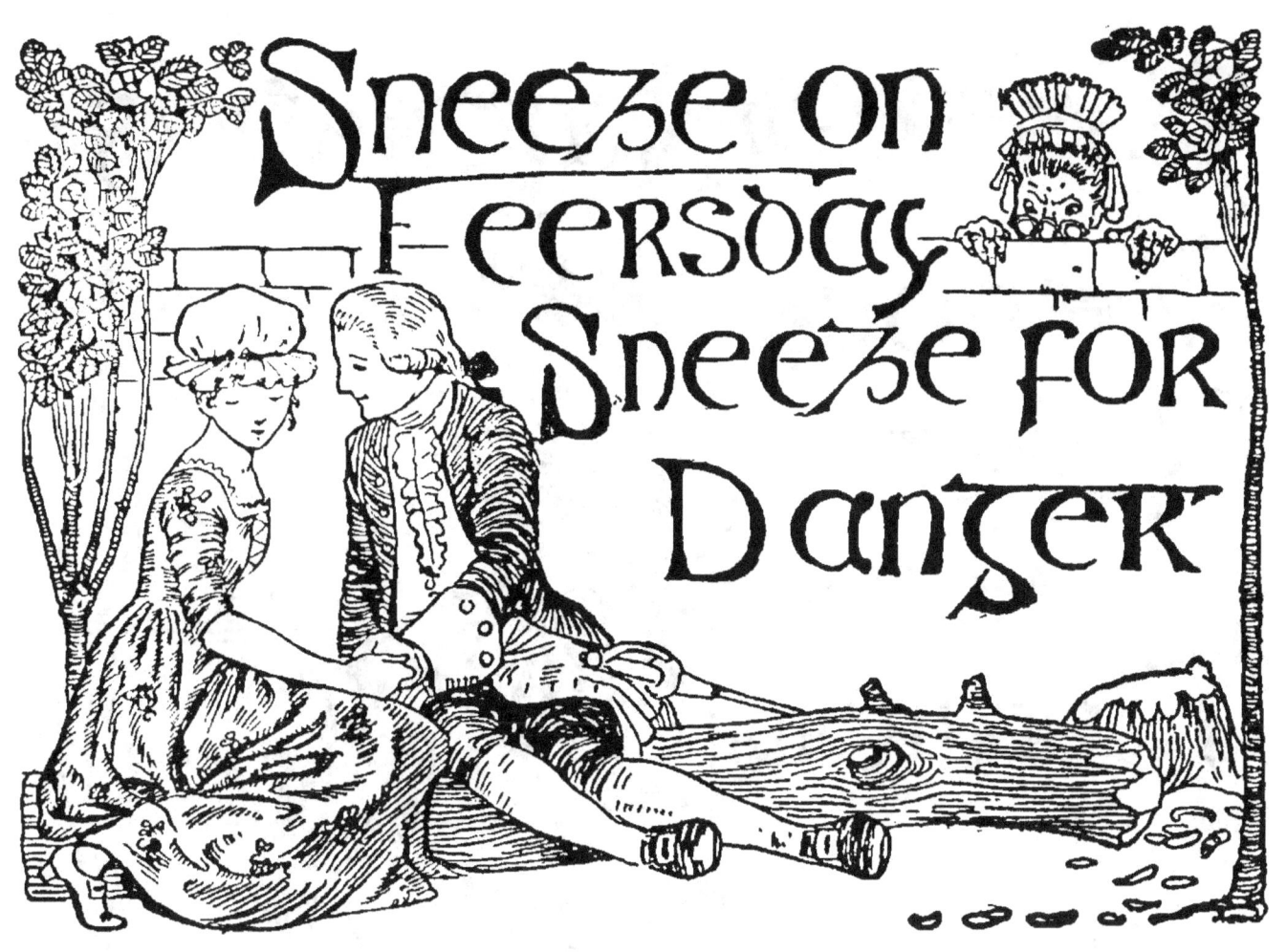

Sneeze on Friday Sneeze for Sorrow

Sneeze on Saturday see your Sweet- -heart Tomorrow

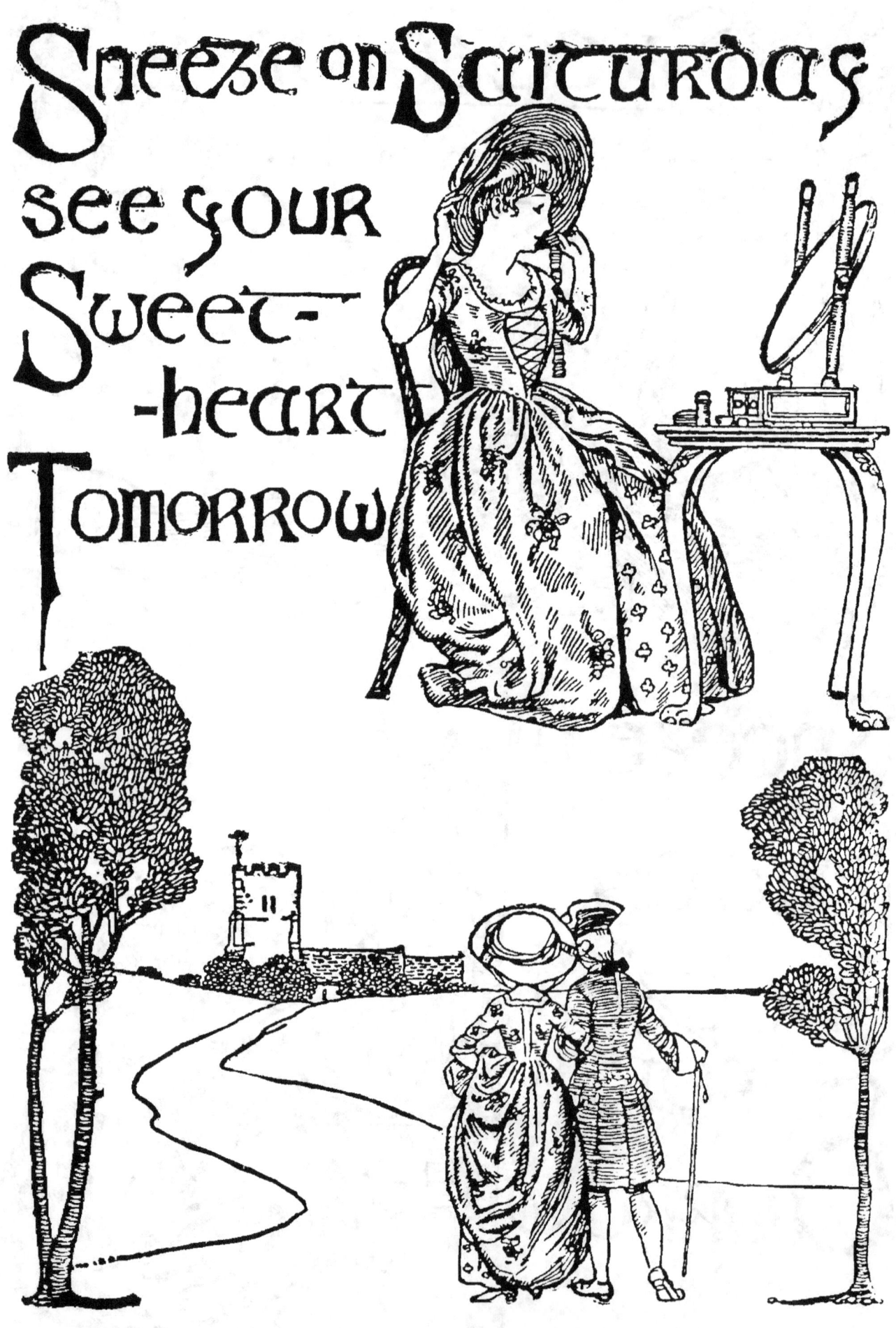

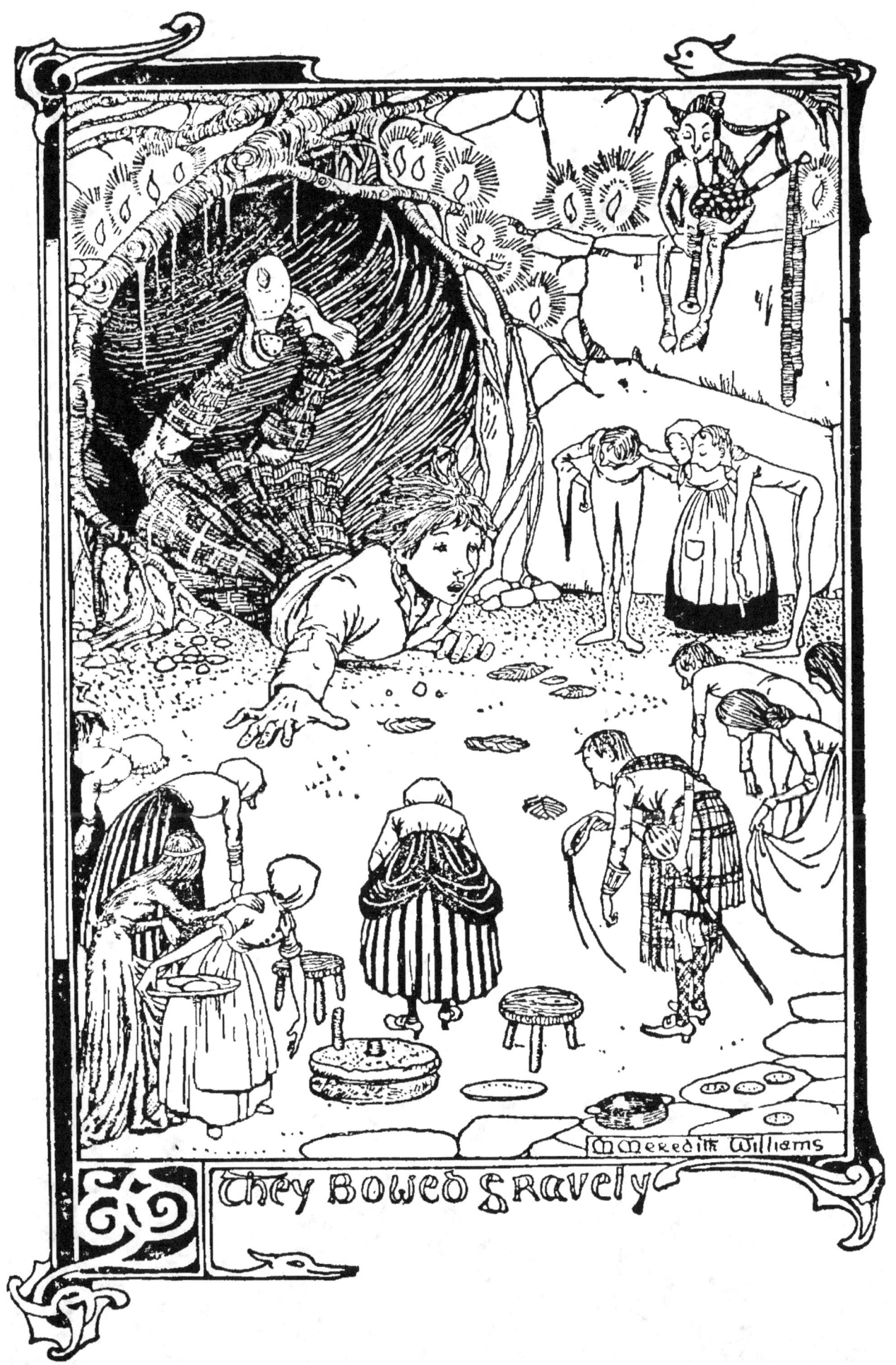

They Bowed Gravely

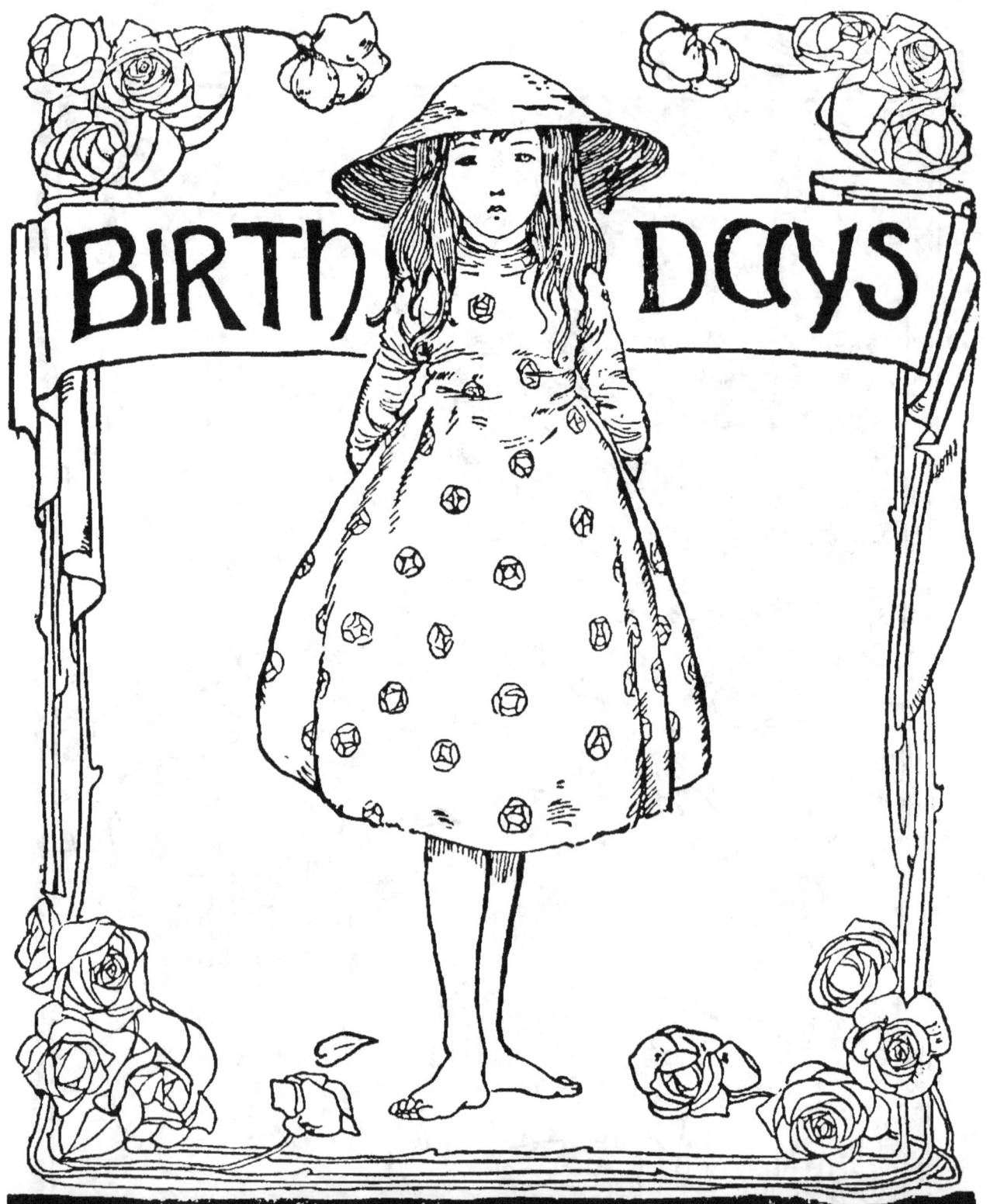

BIRTH DAYS

A Mononday's Child
His a Bonnie Face

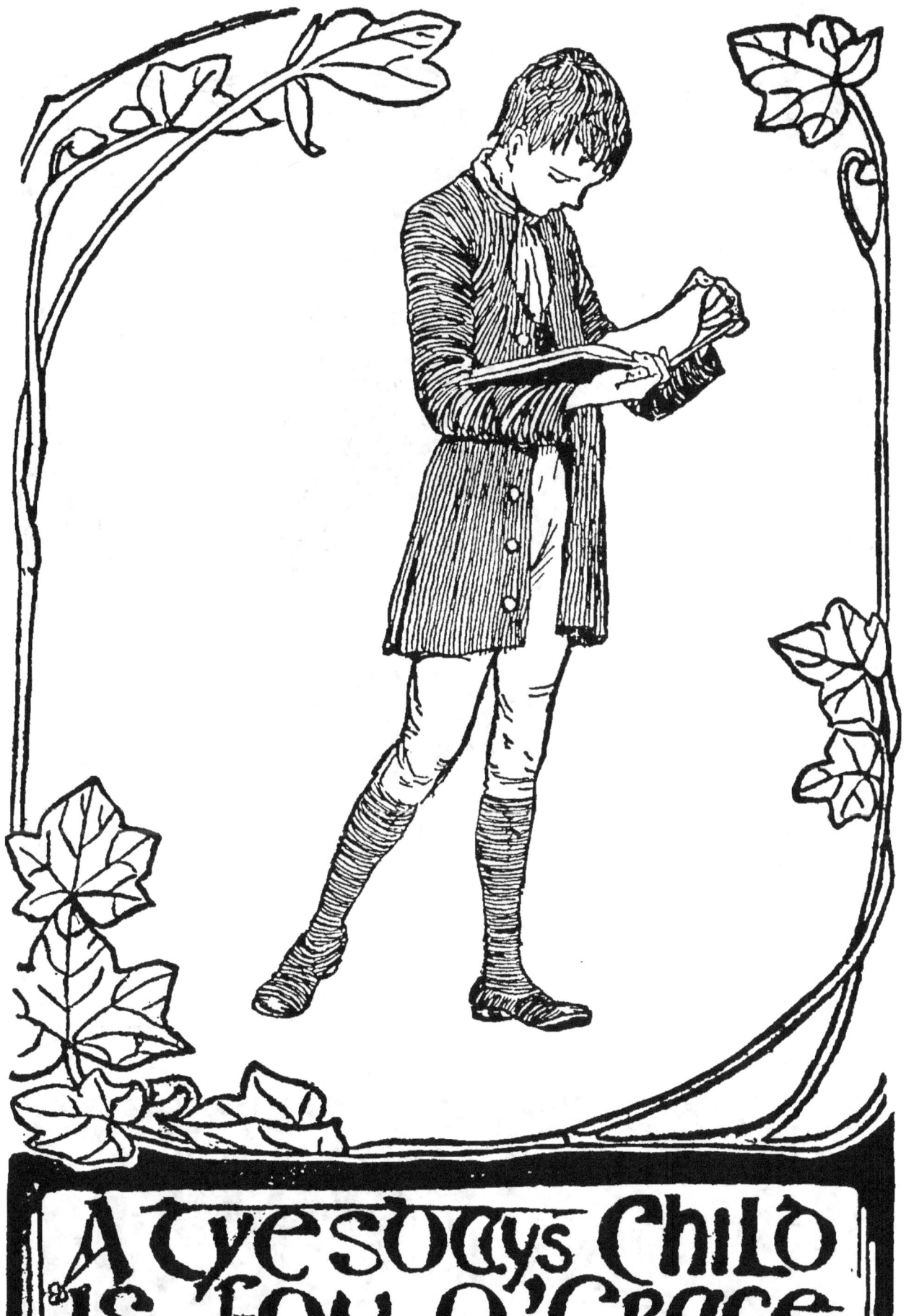

A TYESDAYS CHILD
IS FOU O' GRACE

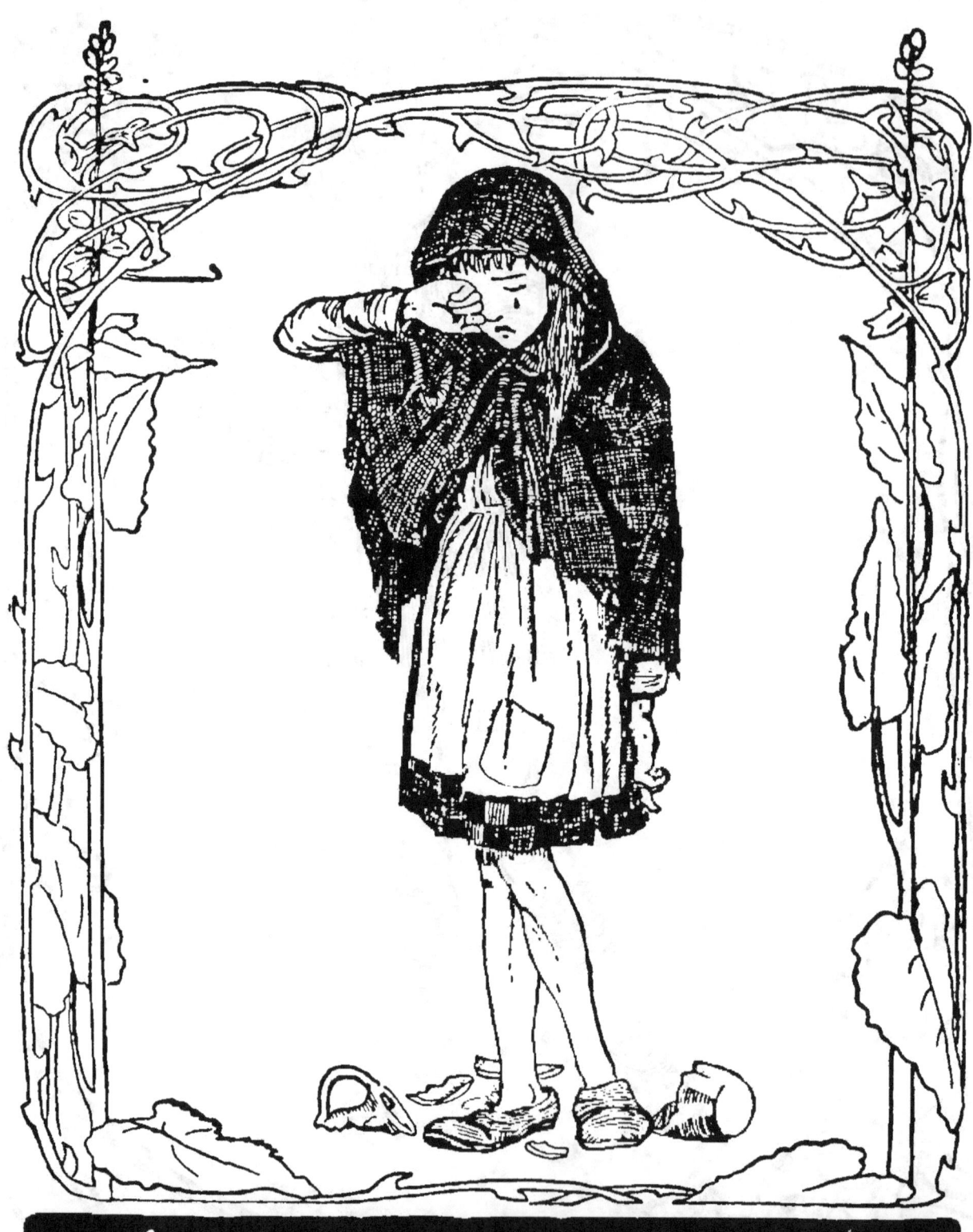

A WEDNESDAY'S CHILD
IS THE CHILD O' WOE

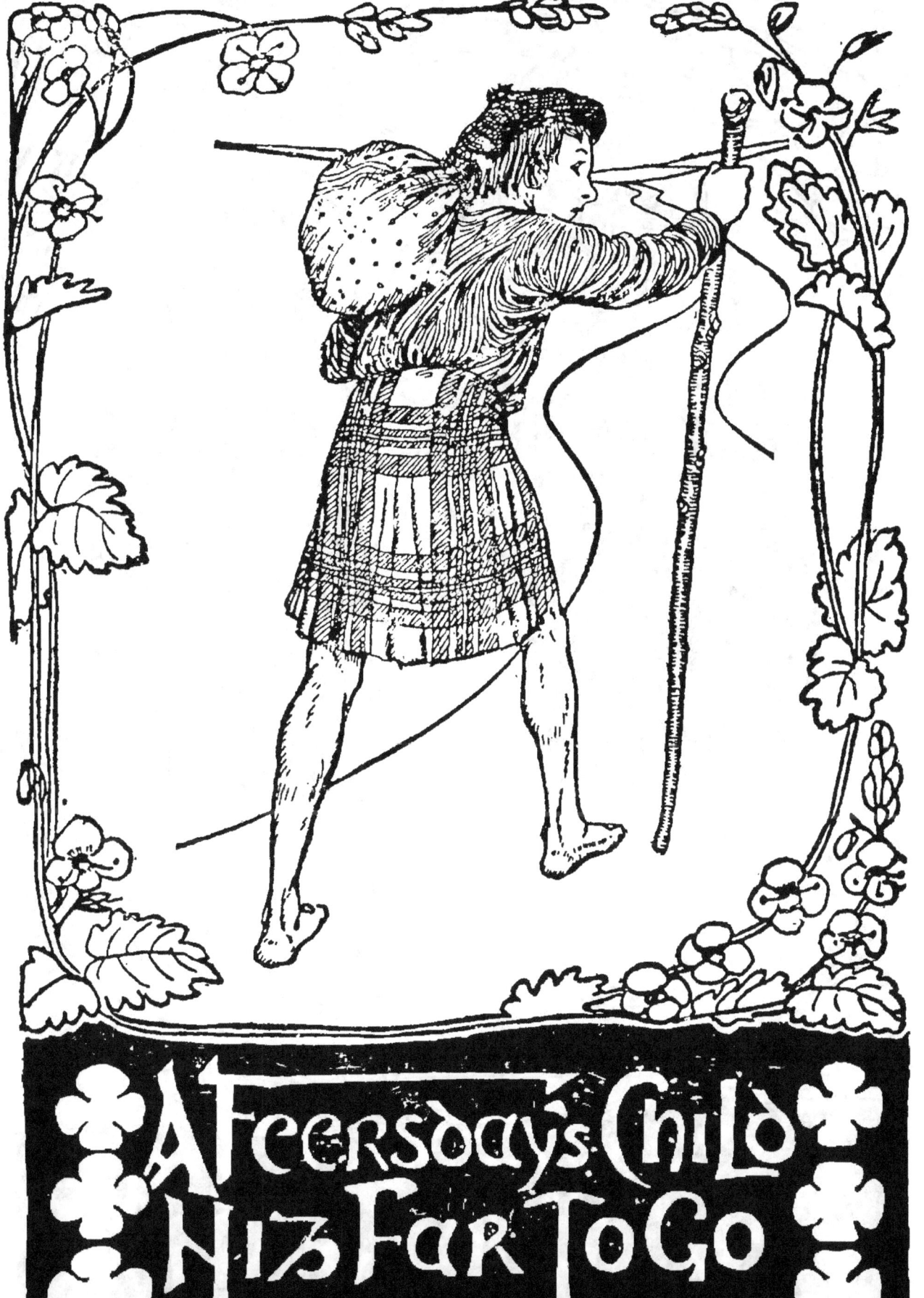

A Feersday's Child
Hiz Far To Go

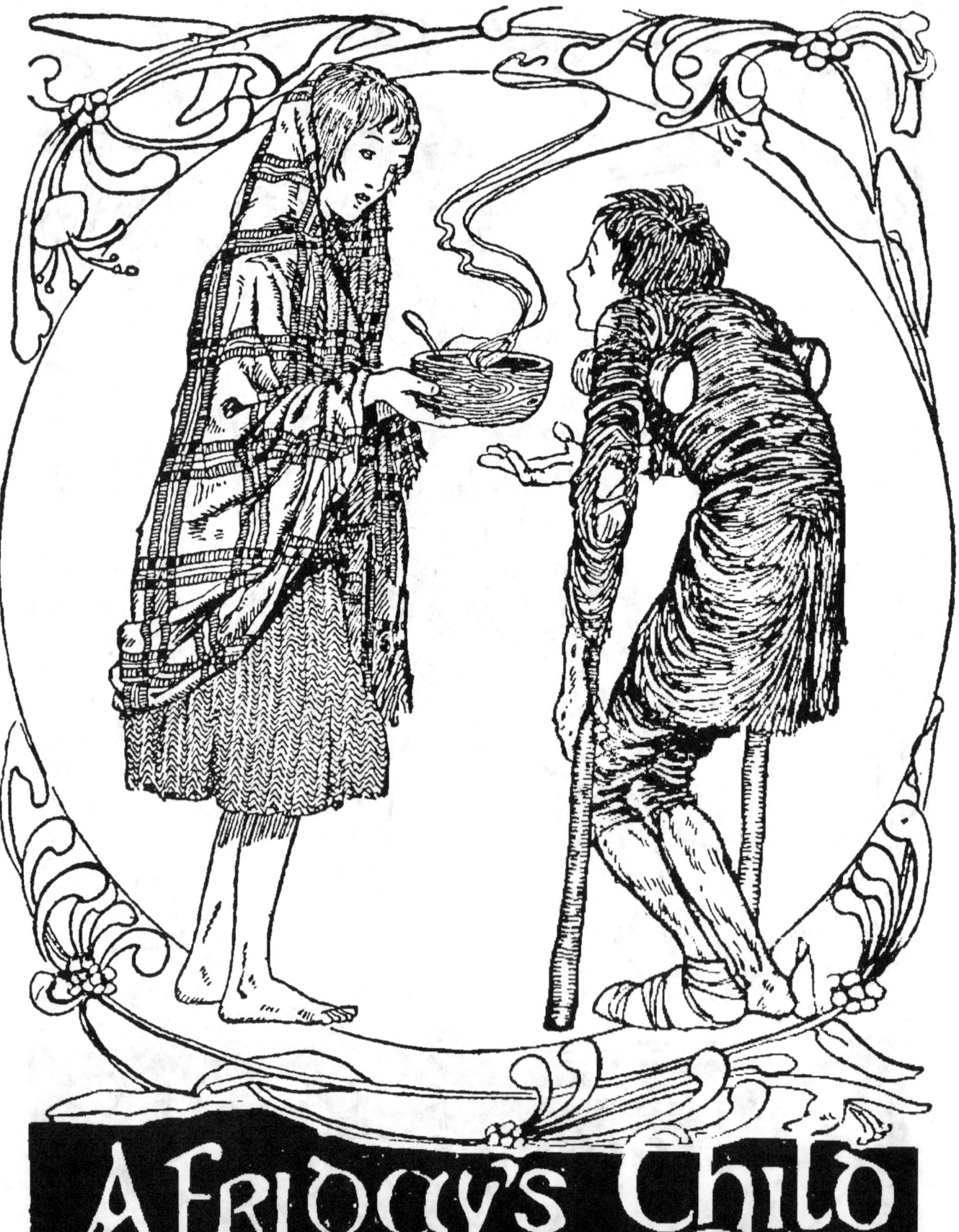

A Friday's Child is Lovin and Givin

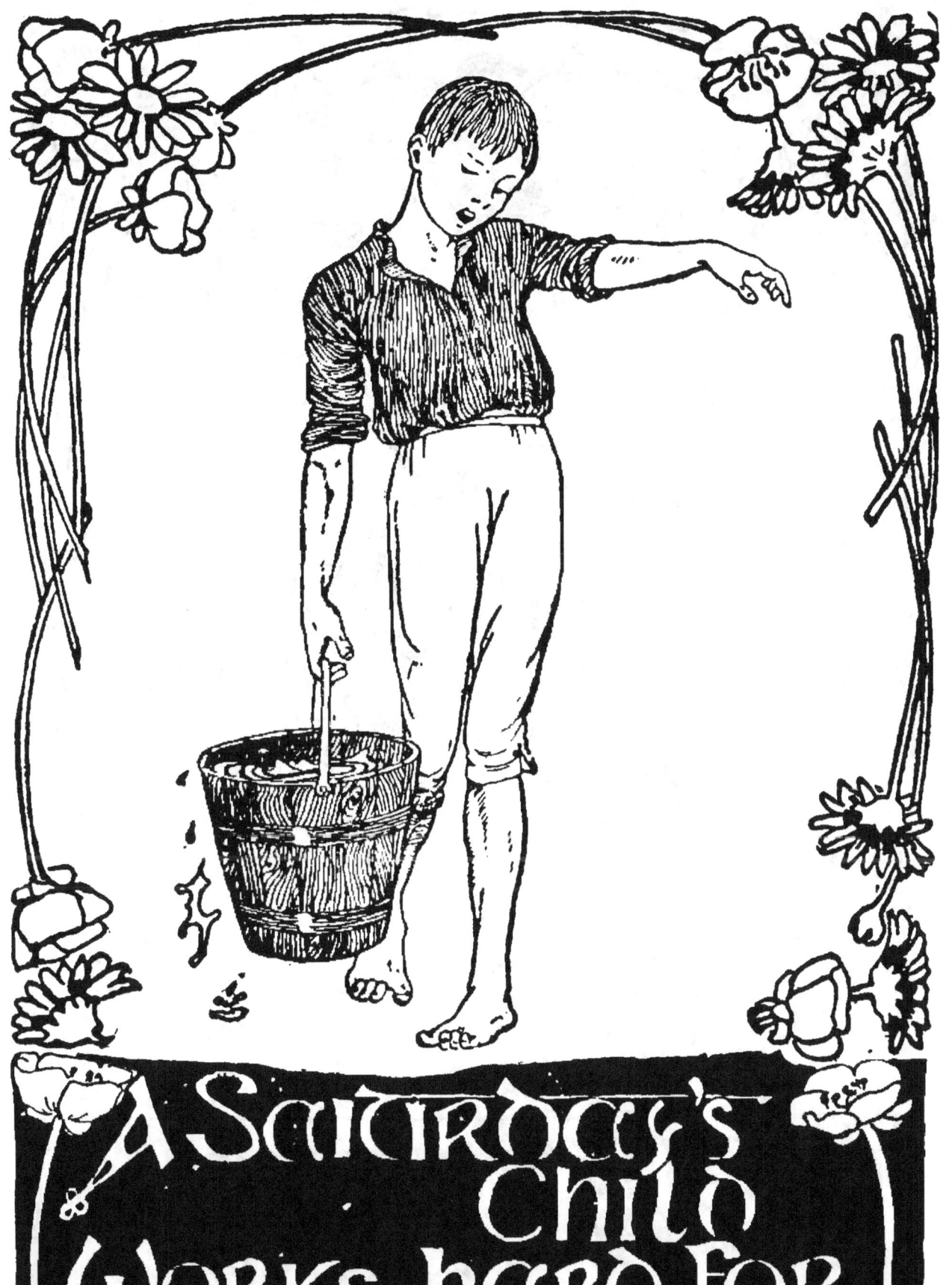

A Saturday's Child works hard for his livin

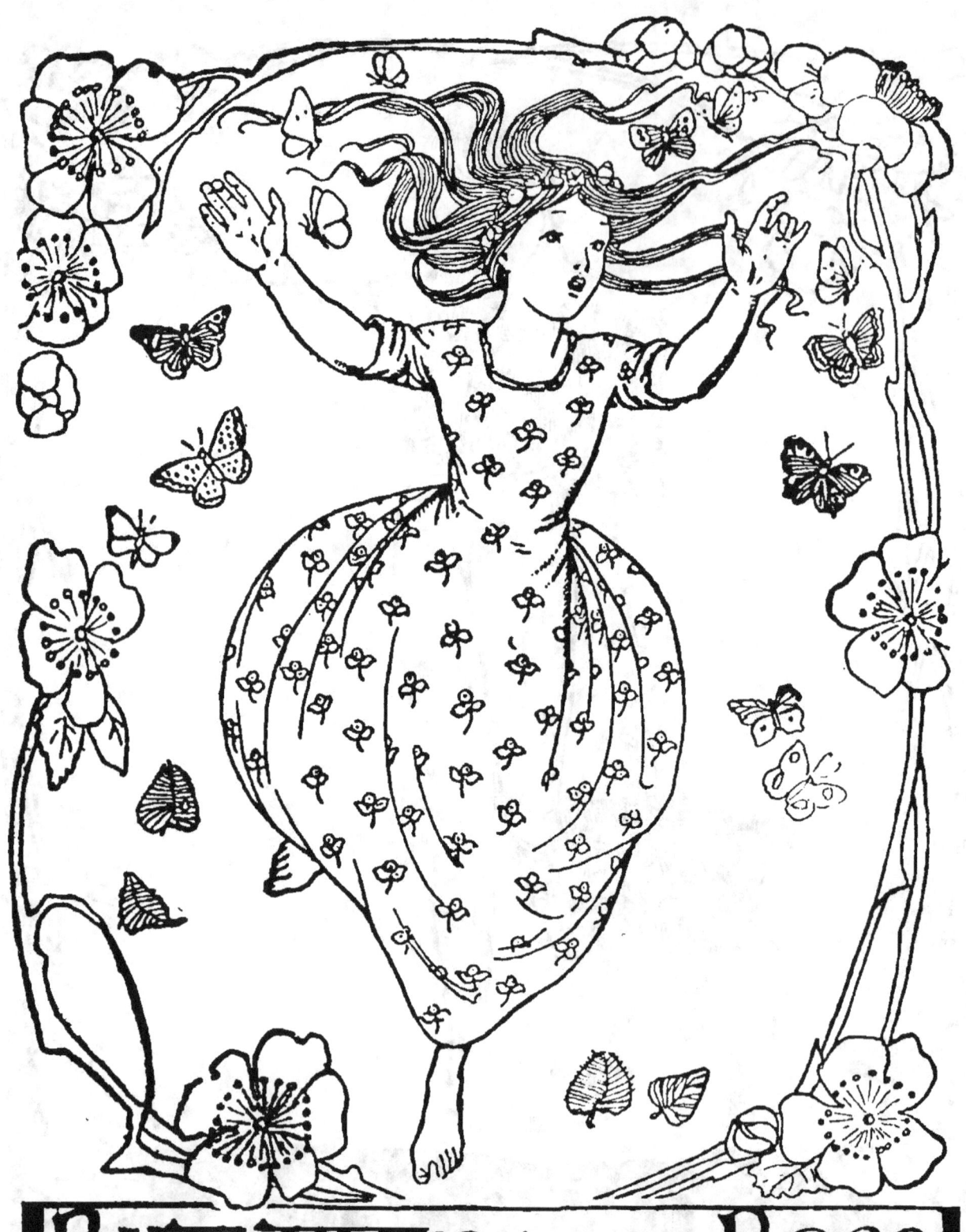

But them that's Born
On Sunday
Is happy, Blithe,
and Gay